ON TOUR

Ralph Moore is a journalist renowned for his contribution to dance music. Starting his journey in the mid-90s, Ralph quickly rose through the ranks at magazines such as *Muzik* and *Mixmag*. He has conducted interviews with legendary DJs and acts such as Björk and The Chemical Brothers, reported from the world's biggest festivals, and provided in-depth analysis of the ever-evolving dance music landscape. Beyond journalism, Ralph Moore is also an artist manager and remix A&R.

RALPH MOORE ON TOUR

A WILD RIDE IN THE DANCE MUSIC PRESS

First published by Velocity Press 2025

velocitypress.uk

Copyright © Ralph Moore 2025

Printed and bound in Great Britain by Clays Ltd, Elcograf S.p.A.

Cover artwork

Hayden Russell

Typesetting

Paul Baillie-Lane

Ralph Moore has asserted his right under the Copyright, Designs and Patents Act 1988 to be identified as the author of this work
All rights reserved. No part of this publication may be reproduced, in any form or by any means, without permission from the publisher

Print ISBN: 9781913231774

Ebook ISBN: 9781913231781

To Mum and her piano – R.I.P. Celia Ann Moore. For the direct line to Mary Tourtel & Alfred Bestall's Rupert Annuals and for the early Tomita - 'Snowflakes Are Dancing' memories from secondary school: I still have them all.

To Jon Fielder (R.I.P.) and Maggie (Hathaway) Kear for making sure I was on the right side of the stage from the very start and to all of Mum's colleagues at Warden Park for being so incredibly kind after her passing in June 2023.

And to absent friends.

CONTENTS

Foreword by Fatboy Slim ... ix
Introduction ... 1

Chapter One: The Saga Begins ... 13
Chapter Two: Finding My Tribe ... 35
Chapter Three: Writing the Wrongs ... 43
Chapter Four: Making Moves ... 61
Chapter Five: Paperback Writer ... 83
Chapter Six: Muzik is the Answer ... 91
Chapter Seven: The End Is the Beginning Is the End ... 117
Chapter Eight: Tiny Dancer ... 133
Chapter Nine: When the Muzik Ends ... 149
Chapter Ten: Moving to a New Manor ... 161
Chapter Eleven: The Can I Get Era ... 173
Chapter Twelve: Freetown Christiania ... 187
Chapter Thirteen: Ice Ice Baby ... 197
Chapter Fourteen: Back to the Balearics ... 205

Chapter Fifteen: (Because You Gotta Have) Faith	217
Chapter Sixteen: Lazarus	223
Epilogue	233
Acknowledgements	237
Pre-Order Thanks	243

FOREWORD

By Fatboy Slim

We were somewhere around Bolney on the edge of Gatwick Airport when the drugs began to take hold…

…a fitting introduction to the rave generation's own gonzo journalist. Ralph Moore's genius in journalism has always been not just to write but to get involved, to live the life. To talk the talk, you have to have walked the walk. He didn't just write the story—he became part of it. Thus, an enthusiastic young scribe grew into not only someone I worked with but also a close friend.

We've both lived through a golden age of dance music. We've travelled together, danced together, and partied together. We've seen things you people wouldn't believe—but Ralph's genius lies in his ability to remember it all and put it into context.

Those who can, do. Those who can't, teach. And those who love, observe…

While the beautiful lunatics Ralph hung out with were instinctively reshaping the music industry, he was the one analysing it and reporting back to the rest of the world through his media work. He was our mouthpiece, our ambassador, our interpreter. We didn't always know what we were doing, but Ralph made sense of it and explained it to everyone else.

From wild adventures at the Manumission Motel to the scout hut in Brighton, from smashing up a hotel in Sydney to watching the dawn break in Buenos Aires, or even just wearing duvet turbans on our heads at the afters at my house—Ralph was always there. He got involved, made us laugh, but, most importantly, he bothered to remember it all and distil it for others.

Like a war correspondent on the front line, he was embedded. Like Hunter S. Thompson, he was part of the story. The real treat is that Ralph also has the conscientiousness and wit to now share it all with us. For those who were there, his words evoke nostalgia. For those who weren't born yet, they offer a glimpse into that most golden age of raving.

Norman Cook
October 2024

INTRODUCTION

Looking back at pictures of my eggshell-blue teenage bedroom wall, I can pretty much see my future sketched out. The main poster, positioned right by my bed, is a black-and-white behind-the-scenes shot from the Pet Shop Boys' promo video for *Being Boring*. The second single from 1990's peerless *Behaviour* album, it marked their first music video collaboration with the legendary (and sadly departed) fashion photographer Bruce Weber. On my wall, Neil Tennant and Chris Lowe are surrounded by all the other main points of my adolescent pop culture reference.

Let's break it down. Alongside that poster, there are shots from David Lynch's *Twin Peaks* and Martin Scorsese's *Dracula*, a 1992 calendar featuring The Cure, and classic band photos of INXS (from their *Kick* era, circa '88, of course). There's also a massive fly poster of Stan Lee's X-Men, illustrated by the then-emerging Korean-American comic book artist Jim Lee. If you look closer at my oh-so-teenage pinboard, nestled among cinema tickets and photos of friends and family, there's a postcard of Scritti Politti's Green Gartside. It's from his still-enjoyable foray into ragga-tinged pop with *She's a Woman*, a dancehall reinterpretation of The Beatles' 1964 non-album single—this time featuring Shabba Ranks. Thirty years later, aside from Shabba Ranks, my own pop life would bring me into contact with every single one of these iconic musicians.

Although very little before or after would come close to acid house in terms of impact on my nascent journalism career, I always think of the summer of '85 as the moment when I truly started paying attention to proper electronic and pop music. That summer's music completely took over my waking life. I was ten years old—too old for toys but still too young for girls[1].

I'd already started keeping an eye on pop the summer before, with formative acts like Frankie Goes to Hollywood and Wham! shaping my early tastes as I listened in my tiny bedroom. But twelve months later, one band would rise above the rest for me—and the world—with the operative word being *World*. In 1985, Tears for Fears became my perfect pop band.

Hailing from Bath, Tears for Fears' two frontmen, Roland Orzabal and Curt Smith, taught me to *listen* through their eight-million-selling electronic pop-rock opus, *Songs From the Big Chair*. The album, featuring just eight tracks, remains a timeless classic, continuing to charm every new generation today. It was a significant leap forward from their debut album, *The Hurting*, which had also been formative for me with its standout singles *Change*, *Mad World*, and *Pale Shelter*.

Aside from *Shout* (which impressively reached number one in America), the Tears for Fears single with the longest tail is *Everybody Wants to Rule the World*. Reissued by Sport Aid in 1986 as *Everybody Wants to Run the World*, the song has found renewed relevance in 2024, capturing the attention of conscious and con-

---

[1] Beyond my homework (equal parts French, German and History and electronic rock and pop), I was trying to be a gymnast most Friday nights in Hurstpierpoint, a small village four miles south of Burgess Hill in West Sussex.

scientious Gen Z pop fans everywhere. In July of that year, it enjoyed a fresh lease on life thanks to its inclusion in the *Minions* movie, *Despicable Me 4*.

Back in '86, the motivation for the Sport Aid reissue stemmed from Roland Orzabal and Curt Smith's decision to skip performing at Live Aid at Wembley the previous summer. Burned out from touring, they viewed the reworked single as a meaningful alternative gesture for charity—and it certainly was.

Originally a last-minute addition to *Songs From the Big Chair*, the song was initially set to include the lyrics "Everybody wants to go to war." This was wisely reimagined into something more nuanced and universal, reshaping the track's 40-year trajectory in both the physical and digital realms.[2]

Since he won't feature again in this book, I want to take a moment to acknowledge the British producer Paul Hardcastle. Unlike Trevor Horn, who dominated 1984 with *Relax* and *Welcome to the Pleasuredome*, Hardcastle delivered what I'd argue was the biggest electronic single of 1985: the anti-Vietnam, anti-war anthem *19*. The Kensington-born composer and keyboard wizard crafted a song that surpassed even the MIDI brilliance of *Everybody Wants to Rule the World* and Duran Duran's *A View to a Kill*. Notably, neither of those British bands reached the top of the UK charts that year.

---

[2] Joe Strummer of The Clash revealed in 1988 that he was in a restaurant and saw Roland Orzabal, where he quipped "you owe me a fiver," stating that the title of *...Rule the World* had been taken from his song *Charlie Don't Surf*. According to Joe Strummer, Orzabal reached into his pocket and gave him a five-pound note, confirming his point precisely and accurately. (I am actually editing this chapter the day after Roland re-married, which makes me very happy indeed.)

As a teenager, America was a country I could only dream of visiting, a place I experienced figuratively through popcorn-fueled, pop-culture-snacking trips to the movies. *19* may not have aged as gracefully as Kraftwerk's *The Model* (no pun intended), but there's no denying its potency and impact. Sadly, Hardcastle never quite recaptured the magic of *19*, though he certainly gave it a good try.[3]

But since we're still rhapsodising about that record, I want to highlight two other examples of its impact. The first—and most inevitable—chain reaction was its immediate parody in pop culture. In the same year of its release, British comedian Rory Bremner, under the name The Commentators, helped create a version of the song titled *N-N-Nineteen Not Out*. This parody focused on the England cricket team's poor performance in Test matches, which I'm told was particularly dismal in 1984.

The second example is more indirect but no less significant: Paul Hardcastle inadvertently helped usher in the rise of the biggest British band of the 1990s that wasn't Oasis. Future Spice Girls manager Simon Fuller never forgot Hardcastle's impact on him. Paul was Fuller's first pop protégé as an artist manager, and Fuller's meticulous nature was perfectly reflected in the name of his first limited company: 19 Management.[4]

---

3 For the benefit of Paul Hardcastle fans – and there are still a fair few out there – that summary of Hardcastle's musical career is possibly a little harsh. As fans of his wider catalogue will attest, the pivotal electro-funk single *Rainforest* miraculously did the business for him in America and helped pivot his synthesizer to (whisper) new age music for the rest of time. (And for any pedants out there, yes I am aware that the song *Don't Waste My Time*, became Hardcastle's second UK top ten in March 1986 but it certainly wasn't number one for five long weeks like '19'.)

4 I never tire of telling this story!

The moving image was in an exciting place in the mid-'80s. Animation and stop-motion were still dominant (the AT-ST scout walker and speeder bike scenes in 1983's *Return of the Jedi* still blow my mind), but something more groundbreaking happened in 1985: the first fully CGI character was created by George Lucas's Industrial Light and Magic team for a little-known episode of *Young Sherlock Holmes*. Technological advancements were propelling culture forward faster than ever, and the Brits were often at the forefront. True to form, that first fully CGI character was—believe it or not—a stained glass knight. And surely, being British, it must have been a knight of the realm!

In 1985, I began to fully immerse myself in music and movies. There were three key reasons for my early synth-pop fascination—and ultimately for my career path and the book you're about to read.

First, the Brits truly had the sound locked down. Whether it was Howard Jones, OMD, or the Pet Shop Boys (*West End Girls* may have flopped in '84 but finally became a bona fide global number one early in '86), it was music that made your feet move and your heart dance. Swap the adjectives around, and the same holds true. For a young kid growing up in a nondescript provincial town in West Sussex, it was also eminently collectible.

On my weekly train trips to Brighton, I'd return from The Lanes and Western Road with cassettes and CDs from my favourite artists. Soon, my musical horizons widened to include Prefab Sprout, Scritti Politti, and anything Prince-related—which quickly came to mean *Love... Thy Will Be Done* by Martika. I still have almost everything I bought back then, and I now refer to it as *the archive*.

The second reason was my cheap but treasured plastic Matsui radio/cassette player from the local Argos. Carefully balanced by the bedroom window, it could just about pick up the impossibly upbeat Capital 95.8 FM, fifty miles away. And if you tuned in at the right time—in '85 and '86, they had Chris Tarrant, *The Network Chart Show* presented by David Jensen, and the returning TV favourite, the prodigal Kenny Everett— you could shake your tail feather to *Dancing in the Street* until the sun went down.

On Capital (or "Capital FM," as the cooler presenters called it), you'd hear early Stock Aitken and Waterman productions alongside Madonna, Level 42, and Brit soul acts like Loose Ends and Jaki Graham. Thirty-five years later, I still can't thank Mick Brown, Pat Sharp, Richard Allinson, and Graeme Deane enough for guiding this lost young soul boy to "Capital Nine Five Eight." It was the first proper club I ever joined—and I didn't even need to leave the house.

Many blank cassettes were filled with new music during those years, and when Pete Tong joined in '88, Capital—like its nearest cutting-edge competitor, Kiss FM on Holloway Road—was championing house music harder than any local estate agent.[5]

And thirdly—and in retrospect, this is probably the biggest factor of all—I was glued to *Top of the Pops* on BBC1 every single week from the age of ten onwards. As I write this prologue in the spring of 2024, I've just rewatched the episode that made a light

---

[5] I still have a tape of Pete playing proper house music on the station in 1990, just a few months before he jumped across to Radio One with an idea called 'The Essential Selection.'

bulb explode over my head back in 1985. John Peel is the presenter, alongside his regular and long-suffering broadcasting foil, Janice Long. Tears for Fears open the show with—oh yes—*Everybody Wants to Rule the World*, with Curt sporting his signature yellow sweater. Peel is hilarious throughout, and it's peak '85, radiating a precious pop feeling I still hold onto.

I've always believed that as an enthusiast of anything, you start in the middle and work your way outward toward the edges. That's exactly what I did as I grew into my teens, discovering cooler club classics along the way by S'Express, Coldcut, and Bomb the Bass.

Thursday at 7 p.m. became a weekly ritual at my house on the Hill[6]—wall-to-wall global pop and rock talent in the studio every week. For a highly attuned schoolboy from '86 to '91, this was *the* place to be. Aside from a very young Vanessa Paradis singing about a taxi driven by someone called Joe (I never caught his surname) and the Euro synth-pop classic *Voyage Voyage* by Desireless, I always found it amusing that European (or as read in your best BBC newsreader voice: "foreign") pop rarely stood a chance with the great British record-buying public.

And I mean that sincerely: the Brits needed their lyrics in a language they could understand, and that was rarely Swedish, German, or French.[7]

---

[6] and it would soon feature another record by Paul Hardcastle called *The Wizard* as the distinctive opening sound bed

[7] *Voyage Voyage*, a teen favourite from the moment I heard it, was a quintessential French disco record remixed by Pete Hammond and Pete Waterman of PWL for the English pop market, making it an incredibly rare French-sung hit,

Week in, week out, *Top of the Pops* was a realistic and powerful snapshot of mainstream music, and I'm happy to say it's now back as a concise time capsule on BBC Four. To this day, I can still tell you where my favourite artists' records peaked in the Top 40 and which labels they were signed to. I'm not ashamed to admit that I soaked up all the details with precision and joy, always wondering how I could ever experience the same rarefied air as the presenters and pop stars on the show.

Gary Davies—whom I would later meet in Ibiza, ironically trying to break into the circuit as a "deep house" DJ—was clearly the coolest member of the *TOTP* team back then. But I also have to shout out John Peel, whose whiplash sparring with Janice Long bordered on prime-time anarchy. And then there was Jackie Brambles, whose cute curly hair and streetwise demeanour did funny things to my insides. She seemed "street" in a way very few women on terrestrial TV came across back then.[8]

For the most part, late-'80s Britain as broadcast on BBC, ITV, and Channel 4 was well-spoken, white, middle-class, and painfully aware of what was going on next door. BBC2 made occasional attempts to explore the fringes, but much of Middle England in the '80s was about keeping up with the Joneses. If you couldn't keep up, the fallback was gossiping about them behind their backs. One-upmanship wasn't as prevalent

---

but over the channel, where there was less resistance to non-English speaking pop, the record reached number one in a further ten countries across Europe. In the UK, it still reached a very creditable number five.

8 Later on she would do a great job interviewing Madonna for Radio 1. I still have that tape in the cassette archive too.

in Burgess Hill, but only because so few people ever managed to escape.

That said, credit is due to the BBC's Alan Yentob for instigating some interesting "yoof" moves. BBC2's *Def II* umbrella was effectively a youth channel within a channel, and it was Janet Street-Porter who introduced British television to hip, youth-oriented programming under its banner. Running from '88 to '94, *Def II* included shows like *Rough Guides*—led by the always magnificent Magenta Devine and her younger co-host Sankha Guha—and the off-the-wall *Rapido*, presented with gleeful irreverence by future French film director and actor Antoine de Caunes.

It's also where I first encountered Normski, a future underground acid house figure and later a popular after-hours photographer of the dance scene.

But—as usual—I digress.

I was a late addition to the Moore family. My sister Elena is nine years older than me and left the nest when I was around 11 to become a hairdresser in nearby Hassocks. My mum, a trained pianist and studious music teacher in Cuckfield, somehow managed to get me into the best school in the county, even though I should have been sent to the more dreary and pedestrian Oakmeeds (now Oakmeeds Community College) in Burgess Hill. Attending Warden Park instead was probably a pivotal educational moment in my early years: it was a great school where I not only thrived in History and English but later took Drama to GCSE level due to my growing interest in theatre and music.

While I didn't play an instrument (I lacked the patience to get past grade five in piano with Mum and had a similarly short-lived attempt at bass guitar), I sang in the choir every week. For the better part of my first two years at Warden Park, I was the butt of Judy Blume *Forever* jokes[9], but that didn't matter—Mum's silent guidance made me a straight-A student, and no amount of teasing could derail me. I'm proud to say I was the first boy at the school to earn an A in Drama studies. While I eventually focused on music and music journalism, part of me still wonders if I could have had an acting career.[10]

My father's part in all of this, sadly, is less positive. He was an angry and strangely emotionless man who never seemed to escape the controlling, ration-driven clutches and ravages of World War II. It permeated his entire life, leaving little room for much else. Never happy with his lot in the planning department at Haywards Heath County Council, he charged around like a bitter civil servant from another era, most evenings and weekends, until I left home for good. Like many raised in what you'd now call *a different time*, he was both homophobic and racist—and fairly proud of it, too. (The *Daily Mail* that landed on our doormat every day played its inevitable role.)

He callously dropped my sister and her partner—later her husband—from his life for having children "out of wedlock"

---

9 In Blume's well-loved (and in many cases life-changing) 1975 novel exploring teenage sexuality, the male protagonist's penis is nicknamed 'Ralph' for some reason. Thanks Judy.

10 The most famous Warden Park alumni from the same teaching collective as me is Game Of Thrones and Star Wars actress Gwendolyne Christie, who also spent five years being taught in Cuckfield: my Mum's best teacher friend Maggie Kear remembers taking her to a modelling agency in the early 90s, where they told her she was 'too fat', even though as Maggie remembers, "she was like a stick! She screamed at them furiously and then stormed out."

(the shame!) and eventually ostracised himself from nearly everyone he ever met, including me. In his will, he grudgingly left me £1,000 (and that grand definitely didn't come for free) and left my sister a beaten-up second-hand car, which she promptly sold for cash. If he were a Roger Hargreaves cartoon character, he would have been Mr. Mean, handing his kids lumps of coal. While my mother loyally stood by him to the very end, when he died, she decided not to attend the cremation. It was as if she'd paid enough penance already. No family tears were shed that day.

Thankfully, my own private universe was expanding, and a knack for finding the right people to hang out with generally kept me on course. At school, I worked incredibly hard to achieve the grades I needed—seven A's and one C (in Mathematics, of course; I'm still fairly hopeless at that). After school, my friends Stephen Brewer and Scott Rolling, who were equally enamoured with the outer fringes of club culture, and I collectively bounced over to Haywards Heath College. There, I studied English, French, and History before heading to Warwick to study English and American Literature.

Something about Warwick resonated with me when I visited the campus for a tour one afternoon. To this day, I'm not sure I'd be writing this book if it weren't for the impact that place had on my decision-making process. Reader, it really was just like heaven—student and campus life at Warwick in the mid-nineties was wall-to-wall wonderful for three glorious years.

CHAPTER ONE

The Saga Begins

As far back as I can remember, I always wanted to be a proper music journalist.

Beyond my love of (quality) pop and crossover acid house hits like Inner City's *'Big Fun'* and 808 State's *'Pacific State'* (which, if memory serves, was the first dance twelve-inch I ever purchased), I was a lifelong pop culture fan and all-round music pedant[1]. I didn't want to work as a clerical assistant or teach English in a school, even though the rest of my family became teachers to some degree, including my nephew Hayden, who taught sport for over a decade in London. I'd grown up reading the pop music bible *Smash Hits*, and by 1989 and 1990, it was covering the sweet spot I loved to a tee: namely everything from Neneh Cherry, De La Soul, and Beats International to New Kids On The Block and a returning Tears For Fears, all with a sense of humour and an ability to prick pomposity—qualities sorely missing from the mainstream rock press. I was only 15 in 1989, so too young, shiny, and new for *NME*'s wicked and vicious games. I was aware

---

[1] Dictionary definition: a person who is excessively concerned with minor details and rules or with displaying academic learning: yep, that's me to a tee

of *NME* and its main competitor *Melody Maker*, of course, but *Smash Hits* was my bi-weekly poster-pullout bible. Without fail, I'd buy it from the local shop in Burgess Hill on the day it came out, and I often stuck those posters and individual lyric pages on my bedroom wall. Exclusive interviews, crosswords, competitions, and free badges would be dissected and mounted, and the features with my favourites would be read again and again as I looked for clues to figure out what was hiding behind their proverbial pop curtains, haircuts, or otherwise. Certainly, at secondary school, music journalism felt like the only realistic route to take if I was going to keep the inner sanctum of my first-floor room alive.

So, it wouldn't be right for this story to start anywhere except at the proper beginning. But where exactly is the beginning of this particular saga? Is it on the stage leading *Cider With Rosie* at Warden Park, playing *Always The Last To Know* by Del Amitri and *Diamonds And Pearls*-era Prince on mid-morning college radio in Haywards Heath? Was it at Warwick University, when I interviewed The Utah Saints, One Dove, and Suede in quick succession within the first year of arriving on campus? Or was it the chaotic five or six trips to Ibiza from the summer of '99 onwards—eye-opening, seat-of-the-pants experiences that, in retrospect, were the ideal *'finishing school'* for an aspiring young journalist who, until then, had been making it up as he went along?

We will start with Warwick.

In September 1993, I arrived at Warwick's Cryfield Halls—CH2 to be precise—as an impossibly inexperienced English student with very little to show for my name beyond a boxful of vaguely alternative CDs and a bagful of what I hoped was boyish charm in my back pocket. I became fast friends with a fellow music and film enthusiast called Tim Plimmer, a brown-eyed boy who lived directly opposite me in those first-year halls. Friendly and fun, this tall, bookish teenager would soon start dating a girl from the same corridor as us called Lynn, making Tim and Lynn the first fully rhyming couple(t) I'd come across. This was a whole new world for me—one that involved food shopping once a week and fending for myself in class or in the pub. None of us knew what was ahead of us in life, so we made the most of life day to day, which in my case meant a mixture of studies, movies, music, and a phone call home once a week.

Campus life offered everything a kid from the sticks could have ever wanted: dirt-cheap beer and lager, a constant stream of live music, and plenty of like-minded nineteen-year-olds eager to explore in every sense of the word. It wasn't long until I fell in love with a girl from Dorset called Anna. The Warwick Arts Centre offered up all the latest films (I can remember devouring *'Jamon Jamon'* during my first term and watching *'Reservoir Dogs'* through my fingers), and it wasn't long until I was made Music Editor of the student newspaper, the *Warwick Boar*.

I can still picture my first-year room. It was relatively small but perfectly acceptable for my basic student needs, and like each Cryfield room in our hall (and there were three different adjacent halls, now and then), it came equipped with a sink, which could be used to wash your face or be royally sick in, depending on the day of the week. I had a cork mood board on the wall to show off my recent indie band tickets—Suede, Primal Scream, and The Smashing Pumpkins among them— and a poster of R.E.M.'s Michael Stipe next to it, shot by my favourite rock photographer, Anton Corbijn. My trusty Sony CD stacking system had made it all the way to Warwick too, as had my carefully curated CD single collection, which I hoped would impress some of my new friends. Next to Tori Amos, you'd find *Weirdo* by The Charlatans and *Groove Is In The Heart* by Deee-Lite. I paid incredible attention to music curation, even at 19. But I really can't pretend that I knew too much about Detroit techno or Chicago house history before I was 20. My experiences of acid house had just about reached Brighton, but only really to big clubs on the main strip by the sea, and nothing beyond what you'd now politely call chart fodder. ²

Warwick University in the mid-'90s was a *fantastic* place to come of age. It wasn't as serious or fiercely academic as the students I'd seen at Cambridge (I'm proud to say that I'm an official Cambridge reject), and it didn't have mediaeval spires or even Victorian arriviste red brick. Instead, it was more of a modern campus uni—but it remains in the UK's Best Universities Top Ten perennially and, like the ubiquitous *Swamp Thing* by The Grid, stayed there snugly for a very long time. Warwick is where the feminist icon Germaine Greer taught as a lecturer (from 1968 until 1973, to be precise), during which time she published her first and most famous work, *The Female Eunuch*. As for the nuts and bolts of the university, it remains organised into three faculties: Arts, Science, Engineering and Medicine, and Social

---

2 When Dot Allison, the Scottish singer from hotly tipped dance outfit One Dove talked to me about the Scottish techno duo Slam, I politely pretended that I knew precisely who and what she meant. I was a mere teen at this point but I swore I'd never let that happen again.

Sciences. But where all the action happened, for me at least, was in two particular places: to the left, as you arrive by road, was Warwick's Arts Centre (where there was a cinema I'd frequent religiously in my first year), and to the right, The Student's Union, where I spent the majority of my time when I wasn't in lectures, chatting to fellow students, playing pinball, or picking up campus newspaper *The Warwick Boar* when it came out on alternative Wednesdays. Although I had never been especially bothered or affected by class, I was vaguely aware that Warwick had attracted a certain strain of Oxbridge rejects. But then again, as I had been one of those myself, I didn't particularly mind or ever feel on the periphery.

I certainly never met anyone I didn't like within my own campus bubble, and the Warwick educational experience was definitely not stuck-up in any way. (It also had a healthy appetite for sport.) I was there to learn, to grow (up), and to get a decent degree. The fact that it was full of people I liked perhaps appealed to my own desire to explore different outlooks beyond the ones I'd seen in the sticks. I was relieved that a few familiar faces had made it all the way from West Sussex to Warwick, including one friend, Helen Broadway, who had done 'the triple' with me, meaning Warden Park 11-16, Haywards Heath College 16-18, and now Warwick University 18-21. (And we are still friends, in semi-regular contact today.)

I'm not going to pretend that I was particularly cool, even though I desperately wanted to be.

That's what the posters and tickets in my room were for. My diet, for example, was a joke. I would buy my weekly box of Pop Tarts and drink endless cups of sugary tea, saving my money for a once-a-week trip to Coventry to see what singles and albums had been released. Still dabbling with grunge and alternative rock, I vividly remember buying Pearl Jam's second album *Vs* (the one with the sheep on the cover!) in Our Price the day it came out and continuing to support my favourite Australian rock icons INXS as they sputtered into the mid-90s. In truth, my sound and vision were fairly mainstream, and I wanted to get away from that. One of the things I hoped Warwick would do (for me) was widen and stretch my repertoire.

The only major DJ/producer who had really come to my attention beyond Norman 'bassline' Cook[3] was the producer and remixer Paul Oakenfold, and that was because he'd remixed and produced *Pills* for The Happy Mondays, whose music I had loved at school, and also because I had seen him supporting U2 on their stadium shows in 1992. By the time I got to college in 1991, I was a fan of the band via *Achtung Baby*, which I still think is a killer rock album that's stood the test of time. Paul's remix of *Even Better Than The Real Thing* gave U2 a hit twice in 1992, and the second time, Paul's remix—which, to be fair, was fantastic and way more muscular musically—had charted even higher than the original version. I'd add Andrew Weatherall as the third, mainly because I'd bought Primal Scream's Mercury Award-winning, Weatherall-produced album *Screamadelica* and had started to see Sabres Of Paradise remixes on lots of artists' CD singles.

---

3 Before *Dub Be Good To Me*, Cook achieved his first solo hit with *Blame It on the Bassline* in 1989, featuring future Beats International member MC Wildski, and I distinctly remember hearing it on TOTP.

CHAPTER ONE: THE SAGA BEGINS

Although he hated the idea of DJs making their way up some kind of career ladder, Andrew wasn't against taking (slightly pointless) major label remixes for a wedge of cash, and who could blame him? After all, he'd been a labourer before becoming a producer, and I can only imagine how different those two worlds felt. One definitely involved more sitting down.

Given the direction my career would eventually take, I should also give a brief mention to another fan of rave who lived at the very end of my CH2 corridor, whose name was Richard. An amiable, dark-haired weekend drinking partner who also loved club culture, we became fast friends through my university years, probably because I spotted a very early Paul Oakenfold mix CD on the table in the corner of his bedroom during Freshers' Week[4]. It resonated with me because the cover featured Paul warming up for U2, which was decades before it became the norm for selectors to warm up for superstars in stadiums.

Looking at the photos from that era thirty years on, I'm struck by how impoverished and pale I looked at 19 — but I don't think diet (or mental health, for that matter) was important to anyone going through university in the early to mid-'90s. As long as we had enough money to buy lager beer (which, incidentally, was never,

---

4 Years later (and I mean many, many rave years later, which may be about fifteen), I actually bumped into Richard at – of all places – fabric in London's meat market district of Farringdon as night slowly turned to day in Room 2. Neither of us were sober but the moment has stayed firm in my mind as it made me ponder how far we'd both come since being campus babies and living together on Park Street in Leamington Spa during our second year of studies. But unlike many of the people who appear repeatedly in this book, I never saw him ever again.

ever more than £1.50 on campus), we were, in every sense, good to go. And if you look at any student photo from 1993 or '94, you won't see a boy without his beer or, in most cases, his plaid shirt.

The internet had started to gently bubble over in the deepest recesses of the library, but in this era — slightly before the mobile phone had become commonplace — we all shared a single landline where concerned parents would do their best to connect with their kids in the evening via the one incoming number. So, if you walked past it and the phone rang, you were duty-bound, as a good citizen, to pick it up and run to the relevant room to see if their son or daughter was around. Let me tell you, I have never experienced a landline ring louder before or since.

Me? I was just happy to be as far away from my (former) home as possible. Home life had become utterly exhausting and monotonous by the time I finished school at 16, with my father's rants about his daughter "bringing shame to the family" becoming almost nightly occurrences. Initially, my sister had two children, my nieces Cherelle and Antonella, "out of wedlock," as my father described them, with her partner Danny, who also happened to be — gasp — black. My father had never been an empathic or understanding parent to either myself or my sister Elena at the best of times, and the arrival of two mixed-race grandchildren did not bring him any joy at all. Sadly, my mum just didn't have the right tools to repair the cracks, so she would constantly fall through them. And that meant home life needed to be put in a box and forgotten about until at least the Christmas holidays.

Although I was born in Brighton and lived for a few years in a quaint village called Ringmer (which is where my very earliest childhood memories stem from), I'd lived most of my teen life to date in Burgess Hill, which didn't have much to recommend it beyond my school friend Steve's independent music shop, Round Sounds, and a burger joint near the station called Uncle Sam's, which is still trading and selling burgers and cheap milkshakes by the train station today. Closer to home — downstairs, most nights — that shouting I mentioned had now become a nightly occurrence. He was a figure from the past, my father: the fast and occasionally furious modern world frightened and angered him, and he mainly took his supposedly misunderstood frustration out on my mother, since I tended to keep out of his way and focused on my studies. I was what you'd call, back then, a 'swot,' someone who wanted to be a straight-A student, and in an ideal world, those grades would get me as far away from West Sussex as possible.

At 19 and on my own in the world for the first time, university represented a chance for sweet freedom. And while I worked hard, I also enjoyed the social aspect as much as the endless English and American Literature essays I had to write and study for. We were all in the same boat, and I hope that remains the same for any student experiencing the university experience today. I never understood the point of studying from home. My father had wanted me to study locally, but I took that to be another attempt at old-school control, so the Midlands was the very definition of meeting them halfway. Besides, my mother always had my best interests at heart, and one open day visit later, I just knew instinctively that this was the place for me.

Warwick was attached at the hipbone to the nearby Arts Centre, and since a small part of my three-year course was film studies,

I joined the Film Club pretty quickly. At a pound a pop to watch a movie, it seemed like the bargain that most social escapades were back then. I also had a Saturday show on the radio, but most important of all, I joined the music team at the uni newspaper, *The Warwick Boar*.

I wanted to do well, but I also wanted to go to gigs, play endless games of pinball at the weekend, and dance to all the acts coming to perform on campus. There was always something to do, especially when you had a sports background (not me in the slightest) or a more creative spirit (100% me, now and then).

I sponged up everything I read, saw, and experienced on the physical plane. This was a golden magazine era for *NME*, *Melody Maker*, and the surrounding print press (*Q*, *Vox*, *Mojo*, *Select Magazine*), and I not-so-secretly dreamed of a job on the News Desk at *NME*, scooping up exciting stories about Oasis and The Stone Roses before teatime. It wasn't just the music these bands made, but also their ethos: they seemed to be having more fun on tour than any of their predecessors from the '80s, and there was a romance to reading about acts heading to America or Canada for the first time. It was an endless world of rock and pop possibilities, and some of these acts — Underworld and The Happy Mondays among them — appeared to have even more fun after the clock struck midnight. They were the very definition of "don't wait up for me."

Looking back, the list of bands I saw or interviewed for *The Boar* is pretty incredible for a fairly shy 19/20-year-old, and a testament to both the music scene in the UK and the uni's draw for contemporary acts. Taking their name from the Nicholas Cage film *Raising Arizona*, British rave duo The Utah Saints (Jez Willis and Tim Garbutt) first came to my attention on *TOTP* but then again during their timely Freshers' Week visit (and they were super-nice, even talking to me at length about that Kate Bush clearance of *Cloudbusting* for their crossover club smash *Something Good*). Then there was the Northern Irish rave act D:Ream (who would soon be number one with their anthemic dance hit *Things Can Only Get Better* and at this point still featuring Professor Brian Cox in their ranks — something they all celebrated together at Glastonbury 2024), and finally the underground Scottish dance act One Dove, probably the definitive dance music interview in all my time as a student journo.[5]

One Dove were a young, soulful indie-dance outfit signed to London Records — which seemed daring then, considering how uncommercial their pop was compared to, say, Shakespears Sister, who'd made it to number one the year before with *Stay*. But they had a singer with pop panache, and the band had been darlings of the leftfield music magazine *Select*, thanks to their cool, techno-leaning credentials and their stellar songwriting skills.

They were 'electronic,' but crucially, they were also in love with classic pop and soul, right in the middle of my own spiritual sweet spot. I mentioned Saint Etienne during the interview as a comparison, and Dot politely pushed back.

Are One Dove a pop group then, Dot?

"Yes, classic pop, your Beach Boys and T-Rex, not your massive advertising campaign. I think what we do is more effortlessly

---

[5] I still have copies of all of these pieces, and the picture in the middle of the book is a snippet of that *Morning Dove White* inspired feature

sincere than Saint Etienne, but Primal Scream I don't doubt. Saint Etienne use clever musical allusions, they're looking to the past solely, whereas we're using our influences from the past and present and hopefully channelling it for a unique sound of the future."

Later in the piece, I ask if London Records have been helpful. (Yes, these really were the kind of questions I asked pop stars at 19.)

"They are," says Dot quickly before stopping. "No, not really," she adds. "They see us as a potential Shakespears Sister. They've given us a lot of equipment but they're just business people, they're not interested in your artistic integrity at all."

One Dove's stories of visiting Rimini, their producer and indie-electronic confidant Andrew Weatherall, and the Glasgow techno label Soma (later home to a nascent Daft Punk) blew my tiny teenage music mind, but it was Dot's innate kindness that really stuck with me, along with the thought and depth with which she talked about her music and career. Now an acclaimed solo artist who has worked with My Bloody Valentine's Kevin Shields and Massive Attack in her own right, there's a slightly faded framed poster of the band's single *Breakdown* signed by Dot and Ian from the band on my living room wall as a reminder of this time. Anyone who loved the band would also experience a slew of classy remixes across the various formats. While the group may have been unhappy with Stephen Hague's shinier single mixes, the double-packs and promotional cassettes featured UK and US remix royalty aplenty: William Orbit, Secret Knowledge, Scott Hardkiss, and even Underworld on their final London single, *Why Don't You Take Me*. Whoever got that assignment knew what they were doing.

In essence, this brave, soulful band opened a window to a world I wanted to climb through and explore... and that brave new world was rave culture.

Beyond the *Melody Maker*-style bands I thought were cool and cutting-edge, Warwick also played host to dozens of future BBC 6 Music legends, from the Talkin' Loud-signed Galliano and 80s upstart Alison Moyet to Tori Amos, The Stranglers, Belinda Carlisle, and... Craig McLachlan. But hey, pretty much everyone at Warwick had grown up watching *Neighbours* on BBC1, so the sight of Craig (I don't recall *Check 1-2* being available that night) singing his huge chart hit *Mona* with his guitar was as good as it got in '95. On Mondays, Warwick had a night called Top Banana, and I am still haunted by the sound of *Boom Shake The Room* to this day.[6]

It was a reminder that on Monday nights, cool and creative took the evening off. And that's something I still experience weekly working within DJ culture thirty years later. Absolutely nothing good comes to fruition before the middle of the week!

I don't remember much about my first Christmas back in Burgess Hill, but what I do know is that Warwick's music bookings got better and better in my second year, with bona fide

---

6 And it was still going until recently, because I checked. "Resident DJs play the cheesiest music known to man for four hours every Monday night!" says the script I found and read online as research, shuddering.

NME-approved pop icons like Primal Scream, The Orb and The Charlatans all visiting our hallowed campus stage, along with a legendary Saturday night appearance from a very young and just-signed-to-Creation Oasis.[7] I was there for all of these shows, and they seemed like a weekly reminder to me that music was the world I wanted to be in, as it moved me in a way that sport and science could not. I was always excited when a new band came along that I could claim as my own, and so many of them passed through university campuses in the 90s. Another good example of a world-class band I saw early on was Skunk Anansie, whose singer Skin I would later meet in Ibiza as a raver in the mid-2000s. ("I enjoyed meeting your brain!" she quipped as she left the party.)

But it was really Oasis who rocked my world, and they had ever since their debut single *Supersonic* crash-landed into the UK charts at number 31. They were hyped to high heaven for their show at Warwick SU in 1993, but for some reason, I didn't chat with them before the gig. I had to wait until 2020 to meet songwriter Noel Gallagher at Tileyard Studios in Kings Cross for a 30-minute interview for Worldwide FM. Noel was charm personified that day, even though I'd been instructed by his PR team not to mention or bring up his brother Liam, which I wasn't planning to do anyway. I turned up (early) to his Kings Cross studio with a copy of *Wilmot* by Sabres Of Paradise in my tight mitts as a musical icebreaker: it worked like a dream, but so did the other two records, which were *Gravity Grave* by The Verve

---

[7] The warm up band was called 18 Wheeler. You are forgiven for not remembering them.

and *Cry Myself Blind* by Primal Scream. I somehow bumped into him again outside his studio after a meeting in Tileyard in April 2024. He was waiting by the door for a package to arrive – I'm pretty sure it was his lunch – and once again, he was very engaging and friendly. But it later dawned on me that I had completely reverted to my excitable 19-year-old self. As Noel's lunch arrived, I told him I'd seen him play at Warwick one Saturday night in 1993, and he immediately smiled and countered with, "We were always good on a Saturday night!"

I spent my first summer vacation from Warwick working for a few weeks at McDonald's at Gatwick Airport, which isn't something I would recommend to anyone. Although it came with a free lunch, that lunch did terrible things to my insides, and I vowed never to go back there again. I think the most positive thing that happened was getting a £5 Our Price voucher one weekend, which immediately went towards a finished copy of *Definitely Maybe* on CD.

For my second and third year, I opted to live in Leamington Spa rather than nearby Coventry. Leamington Spa had nice parks, a good high street, and plenty of cheap Balti houses, where for £2.50 a pop, hungry students could fuel up. Between my second and third year, I took a job at Woolworth's in the summer, as it meant I could stay completely away from my parents' increasingly tense home life and still be home in time for *The X-Files* in the evening. The only thing missing during the summers was the camaraderie of campus life, which, in term time, meant live music every week and a multitude of friends to drink lager with.

So, while I enjoyed writing about music for *The Boar*, I also worked hard on my essays and read literature from Toni Morrison

(*Beloved*), Edith Wharton (*The House of Mirth*), *The Edible Woman* by Margaret Atwood, and Zara Neale Hurston's *Their Eyes Were Watching God*. These books remain on my bookshelves along with all my key autobiographies. I never, ever missed lectures as a rule — even at school, I only missed one day due to sickness in five years — but I also never missed a major social occasion or a movie screening. At that age, movies, just like music, can affect you deeply, and I remember seeing *American Graffiti* one Friday night at a midnight screening and coming out feeling… different.

What was it that made this *Graffiti* stick? It might be that it captures the zeitgeist of the 60s and reminded me how far we've come. It also captures an innocence about America and its teenagers that would soon be lost, and perhaps that's what I was yearning for, as well as looking forward to losing a bit of innocence myself. It was set in 1962, when the radio was powered by personalities like Wolfman Jack (perhaps the closest America got to John Peel), and he even beamed down to earth to make a brief appearance in the film himself.

Everything about the film spoke to me, from Ron Howard as the main protagonist to the music and the look of the film, which captures what it was like to be a teenager back in 1962. That, I decided, was the power of a great producer and director, and to this day, I'd say this is my favourite George Lucas film that isn't *Star Wars*.[8] But it was the movie's themes that hit me like a rock: the film depicts multiple characters coming of age, such as the decisions to attend college or whether to live in a

---

8 Film fans will already know full well that he didn't direct *Empire* or *Return Of The Jedi* although he remained a back seat driver.

small town. At its core, the film's Main Street setting represents the nearing end of an era in American society and pop culture. I particularly loved George's choice of songs for the film, like Chuck Berry's *Almost Grown*, *The Book of Love* by The Monotones, and *Surfin' Safari* by The Beach Boys. Still 19 when I saw it, the movie hit me in the same way that *Reservoir Dogs* and *The Piano* would later, in equally seismic fashions. In other words, a brilliant ensemble cast, a director with a vision, and a soundtrack or carefully curated song list that would stick with you emotionally long after the movie's plot had dissipated from memory a few months later. [9]

As a result of seeing *Graffiti* so much, I later went on to watch a couple of in-depth, in-person conversations in Brighton and London with producer Garry Kurtz, who sadly passed away a couple of years ago. Back then, it was a coming-of-age movie that arrived at just the right time for me, and for movie fans, it's the first (and last) time Harrison Ford cruises the strip on celluloid. [10]

But beyond the movies, campus was mostly about music for me. I remember smoking weed backstage with Alex Paterson from The Orb before their live show one Friday night in May '95, and I distinctly remember seeing Norman Cook wandering around

---

[9] There was only one other movie soundtrack from the 90s that I'd say trumps all others of the era, and it's Cameron Crowe's *Singles* soundtrack. Not only does the film feature Eddie Vedder from Pearl Jam, it also features *State Of Love And Trust* - an all-timer from the band - and *Drown* by The Smashing Pumpkins. Like Quentin Tarantino and to a certain degree George Lucas and his team, I was drawn to directors with great taste in music.

[10] Thank goodness they didn't bend to executives who wanted to call it 'Burger City'.

Warwick campus when Freak Power came to town just months before *Turn On…* went gold on the UK singles chart. Little did I know how much of the world we would later bond over together or what an amazing human he'd turn out to be. Beyond the main stage, I witnessed formative DJ gigs from the likes of Sister Bliss (I loved the epic, trance-tinged dance label Cheeky that Rollo from Faithless had launched) and caught mid-career college gigs from the likes of Todd Terry, who was reputed to have been paid £10K to play a very predictable two-hour DJ set. Whenever there was a club night of note—and over the three years, we'd watch everyone from Apollo 440 and Fluke to the world fusion dance collective Transglobal Underground—I was mostly accompanied by another rave-fixated friend from Romford in Essex named Russell Davis. We'd met and bonded during the first night of Freshers Week over a love of—who else?—the DJ and producer Andrew Weatherall.

So, I was an indie kid who got caught (or should that be tripped) up with Primal Scream's *Screamadelica*, *Weekender* by Flowered Up, and anything that The Dust Brothers turned their hand to remixing. And while Tears For Fears' first two albums had soundtracked my teens [11], The Smashing Pumpkins took that mantle after seeing them live at Brixton Academy with my indie-fixated, shaggy-haired Warden Park School friend Scott rolling on my 19th birthday. The support act? An emerging Virgin Records-signed act called The Verve, whose early psychedelic music accompanies me to this day. If it was melodic, tripped-out, and soulful, I simply wanted in. I should also give a shout-out to

---

11 (their third album *The Seeds Of Love* came out on my 16th birthday, FFS)

the incomparable singer/songwriter Tori Amos, who signed my entire CD collection before playing Warwick Arts Centre in the spring of 1994. I also got Tori to sign autographs for all of my friends. "Give them an inch," growled her tour manager John Witherspoon after soundcheck, "and they'll take a mile." It was simply another window—or parallel universe—that I wanted to climb into. And on a good day, I still do.

I really didn't experiment beyond that spliff experience with Alex Paterson at University, but I became friends with all of Russell's first-year corridor (who I secretly felt were way more fun than most of mine) and took Anna on an early date to see Tori Amos at The London Palladium, which at the time felt like a big step towards twenty-year-old maturity. Alas, in reality, I was still a kid figuring out his way in the world – but having a girlfriend helped my confidence enormously, and having written a variety of think pieces for the paper, I soon became the full-time Music Editor of the *Warwick Boar*, commissioning reviews about Pulp and The Pasadenas from pop culture vulture and future film critic James King and his buddy, the always amusing Stephen Merchant, neither of whom need much introduction, especially Stephen.[12] When Anna spent a year out in Siena for the second year as part of her Italian degree, I would visit regularly and vice versa. By this point, we were too entwined to break up despite the crazy distance. Letters, postcards, and phone cards kept our communication lines open – since very few, beyond Cambridge scientists,

---

12 This is the very last time I'll mention this I promise but it's true: I still have all the print copies of the best issues I worked on, although for sanity and space-saving, I've recently downsized from two to one.

used email regularly yet. That was the sweetest and cheapest way to update each other. I'm amazed we stayed together, though I was never one to stray.

Then as now, music and the arts drove the agenda of everything I did. There are still records that, if they pop up, will always remind me of those magical halcyon campus years. Three in particular by The Smashing Pumpkins – *Cherub Rock*, *Tonite Tonite*, and *1979*. Primal Scream – *Rocks* and *Cry Myself Blind*. One Dove – *Fallen*. Oasis – *Live Forever* and, even though I lost £5 on a punt that it would be Christmas number one, the string-driven single *Whatever*. Anything and everything Andy Weatherall touched in this era, but especially *Morning Dove White*, *Wilmot*, and *Theme* from the long-forgotten Brit film *Shopping*. Blur – *Girls and Boys*. And Galliano's *Twyford Down*, although I refused to go and see them perform because, unlike Anna, I didn't want to pay seven – seven! – pounds (I still stand by that budgetary decision). There was also an absolutely magic second-hand record stall that came to campus every single Wednesday, and I devoured its contents every single week. I still remember the excitement of buying a D:Ream double pack (my very first double pack!!) for £3, which I cherished then and still play now. It featured remixes from the UK and the USA by David Morales and Sasha (the closest I'd got to Sasha before was my trainspotting school friend and future record shop boss Stephen Brewer playing me his remix of Urban Soul's *Alright* when I lived in the sticks). I also bought another Smashing Pumpkins compilation called *Pisces Iscariot* in 1995, and on it, Billy Corgan covered *Landslide*, many years before the Fleetwood Mac song would achieve immortality for a third time via a viral TikTok moment that helped bring their music to a new generation. When D:Ream went to number one the second time around with *Things...*, it felt like a major victory for the world I wanted to inhabit – and so did the Labour Party, apparently, who used it to soundtrack Tony Blair's election victory in 1997. In retrospect, it's a wonder I didn't persevere with a musical instrument of my own to play (Mum gave up teaching me piano at grade five, as I briefly mentioned), but my curiosity to learn and engage with the art form was enough. Not unlike the three original factors that powered me straight out of Mid Sussex, the other thing that I learned early on was that press officers in London would send you records and offer you prizes and tickets to shows if you picked up the phone and listened to them. To this day, I am slightly annoyed that I missed Jeff Buckley in Birmingham... but boy, did I not miss the big one.

CHAPTER TWO
FINDING MY TRIBE

Early in 1995, following a casual invitation from the press team (if memory serves, they were called Beatwax), Russell and I embarked on an 18-hour adventure that would change the course of my life. On May 6, 1995, we took the train to Oxfordshire and entered our very first rave: Tribal Gathering. It was the biggest organised electronic music event in England that year.

My school friend and Pet Shop Boys superfan Stephen—affectionately known as "Brewer"—had already regaled me with stories of his trips to Sterns, the (fairly) local Worthing rave mecca, where he'd seen Carl Cox. But now, at 20, I was about to experience The Prodigy, The Chemical Brothers, Moby, and Plastikman for myself. In the jungle tent, we discovered Kenny Ken. The lineup was—and still is, nearly three decades later—utterly incredible, setting the tone and direction for the next 25 years of my life.[1]

The headliners were Orbital. While the lineup was dominated by male artists—a trend that would persist in electronic

---

[1] (Promoter Vince Powers, whose life was tragically cut short at 76 as I wrote this chapter, played a huge part in the success of this Gathering with co-promoters Universe.

music globally for a very long time—Tribal Gathering featured one female DJ: Singapore-born techno producer Gayle San. Her name stood out on the poster then and still resonates now. Like Carl Cox, she was known for her mastery of playing on three decks. She later held a residency at the legendary Omen club in Frankfurt, as well as at Club UK. In short, she was an early dance music pioneer who truly deserves her flowers.

What's the best way to look back on Tribal Gathering now, from the comfort of my home in Hackney? That all-nighter at the rave truly changed my life.

It didn't hurt that it was a beautiful day for the *Muzik*-sponsored Gathering in Beckley. Recently, I found some footage of the festival on *The BPM Selection* channel on YouTube before starting this chapter. Happily, my memories of the night align perfectly with what I saw in the video, rattling contentedly in my nostalgic memory box. The audience was predominantly white and about 80 percent male, but there were still plenty of girls. Almost everyone there fully embraced the raver identity, sporting signature whistles, "Just Do It" T-shirts, and a fair share of sweat-soaked, shirtless enthusiasts.

I distinctly remember the gritty, electric energy of the jungle tent and how effortlessly cool the crowd seemed. The style of the day was on full display—Stussy, Nintendo, Ellesse, and Umbro dominated the fashion choices. I can still evoke the exhilarating feeling of freedom and joy I experienced standing next to a guy in a Meat Beat Manifesto T-shirt. Carl Cox, CJ Bolland, Billy Nasty: this was techno before it became businesslike, acid before it softened into house. Like *American Graffiti*, it spoke to me in a voice louder than any record by Culture Club. It hinted at a way of life far more exciting than anything I'd known.

CHAPTER TWO: FINDING MY TRIBE

It certainly helped that we were outdoors, in a field far removed from anywhere, with hot running water and endless energy. But the music was the real magic—wall-to-wall brilliance, cutting-edge and hardcore in the best sense of the word. It was a world apart from the high street-supported house scene I'd seen in Sussex.

Beyond The Chemical Brothers and Moby, the act that captivated Russell and me the most was The Prodigy. Part of the appeal was that Russell hailed from Romford, not far from Braintree, where Liam Howlett and the band were from. Formed in 1990, The Prodigy emerged just as pop and rave began to intertwine, producing early club hits like *Charly*. By the time their second album dropped, with the incendiary *No Good (Start the Dance)*, they'd accidentally become superstars. The track encapsulated the raw, rebellious energy propelling rave culture to ever greater heights. Liam and Keith, with help from Maxim and Leeroy, were characters in their own movie—complete with a plot, a soundtrack, and an unmistakable identity. They gave great copy and famously gave zero fucks, a spirit that resonated deeply with their audience. "Fuck 'em and their law," growled Maxim in one of their most iconic mantras. The Prodigy were fast becoming superstars, yet they remained unapologetic outsiders.

That feeling of freedom surrounded The Prodigy—it was embedded in the music of The Chemical Brothers and Orbital too. The sound was too cool to be mainstream yet too big to be held back. Monumental in ambition but mistrustful of MTV, it retained a countercultural edge even as it hurtled toward ubiquity. In a word, it was *potent*. For a while, you could be cool and have the tunes to match the mindset.

The issue only arose when acts made a dash for the mainstream or sacrificed their initial authenticity for higher chart positions—a pitfall arguably exemplified later by The Shamen. [2] But for now, that freedom came from dancing with like-minded people, sharing thoughts and beliefs, and collectively savouring the signature moments of songs and techno instrumentals. It was about remembering the wave of emotion that would wash over you, uniting everyone in the room.

Was techno my new religion? To me, it seemed that electronic music spoke far more directly and truthfully than any religion ever could. And no record captured this new sense of possibility better than David Holmes' remix of The Sabres of Paradise's *Smokebelch*. Wherever I went, it felt as though Weatherall's invisible production touch was following me. Decades later, it still does.

Yes, I was shook, and that rave – split into tents called Starship Universe, Planet Of The Cyberpunks, Tribal Temple, Erotica and Planet Nexus - fairly split my head in two. It was also the first time I'd heard proper techno at that volume and intensity.

Jungle was peaking (not to mention massive) in 1995 and hardcore/breakbeat culture was still prevalent in many of the tents but what I see now in the YouTube footage is acts getting their shit together to play live, or at least as live as their humble setups would allow. The jungle DJ Kenny Ken took no prisoners (and like so many, is still cooking today) and everyone's t-shirts were soaked

---

[2] That's not a proper diss on The Shamen per se, more that as these acts grew in stature, the labels they were signed to, as we saw from Dot's comment about London, sought to capitalise on their early success and broaden their appeal to a wider market, often via remixes. But this was all to come.

through with sweat. "This actual rave here is like the old times because it's still got the vibe," says Kenny Ken on the YouTube clip, which is almost an hour long and well worth tracking down. "But things have changed, yeah. Abroad… they're a few years behind. And basically they're just copying everything we've done. In Canada, they're starting to make music. And they've made a few jungle tracks in Germany. They're very keen to get involved!'

Ken's set that day was a mixture of jungle, drum 'n' bass and hardstep and later - much, much later, as the sun was rising - I can remember hearing Richie 'Plastikman' Hawtin drop *Spastik* as well as Orbital's cheeky nod to Belinda Carlisle's *Heaven Is A Place On Earth* in the middle of their headline set. This was the sound and vision of an industry exploring and formulating a new identity in front of my very eyes, and the Tribal Gathering team did something that's still rare today; they'd put together a world-class bill with the emphasis on quality techno and rave rather than rampant fluffy bra commercialism. It was a vibe, it was a bona fide club community and I immediately felt at home with the music and the crowd. There were compelling performances everywhere you looked. Moby was by this point a star and as well as his Twin Peaks theme-sampling chart hit *Go*, he could also challenge the crowd with a bonkers track like '1000' which, as fans will know, is a BPM reference that's reflected in the record itself. Iconic French DJ and producer Laurent Garnier was there too; the equivalent of a premier league striker in 1995, he gave us *The Man With The Red Face* in 2000[3] and remains a top tier club proposition today.

---

3 Though my favourite breakfast snack of his remains *Crispy Bacon*

Around 30,000 clubbers attended that event, and some of us never took off our dancing shoes again. As press representatives, Russell and I had backstage passes, allowing us to observe the artists as they arrived and interacted. For me, this access was the icing on the cake. I wanted to understand how everything connected: the framework of the festival, the choice of records each DJ played, the logistics of paying these artists, and how they'd achieved a spot on this Tribal Temple lineup. And how, in a pre-digital world where faxes dominated communication, they managed to make a career out of it all.

It certainly didn't hurt that the scene felt like a bona fide community, complete with its own dress code and a uniquely underground perspective on the outside world. Sometimes, I think early acid house and rave culture suffered the same fate as football when the Premier League—and big money—took over. But back then, what we were experiencing was something far more important than financial gain. The deeper I delved, the more I realised that the countercultural, experimental electronic music world was a space I needed to be a part of. It felt like home—a place where some of the greatest moments of my life would unfold. And yet, it was just the beginning. If documenting the scene from the inside was my way in, then so be it. I wanted to ask the questions I'd want answered as a fan reading at home on the sofa, without rattling the DJs or producers I interviewed.

That day, I casually chatted with members of Sunscreem—a house music outfit from Essex known for their *Boys Own*-powered hit *Perfect Motion*—as well as Liam Howlett from The Prodigy. But one of the highlights was meeting Tom Rowlands and Ed Simons of The Chemical Brothers in person for the first time. Tom, the taller, more laid-back producer, and Ed, the dark-haired, always-curious acid house fanatic, immediately struck me as an intriguing duo. Always armed with a nerdy question, I asked why they had just signed with Virgin Records for their debut album. "We just wanted to be on the same label as Mike and the Mechanics," quipped Tom.

Since then, I've followed their career closely, watching them evolve from Dust Brothers to chart contenders and now, arguably, the most consistent and celebrated British electronic duo of their generation. Their meticulous attention to sonic detail, innovative video content, and groundbreaking live production have made them truly multi-generational pioneers. While their potential was evident in 1995, few at Tribal Gathering could have predicted just how far they'd go.

As we left Otmoor Park in Oxford, Russell and I picked up the first issue of a brand-new dance music magazine. Coincidentally, Tom and Ed graced its cover. It was called *Muzik*. Fuelled by around twenty cans of free Red Bull and a boatload of adrenaline, we made our way back to college on zero sleep. At the time, I had no idea that this 24-hour whirlwind would take me from a sleepy town in West Sussex to pivotal electronic events in Australia, Singapore, Miami, Ibiza, and South America over the next two decades. In 1995, *Muzik* was just a magazine to read on the train home.

Tribal Gathering taught me several things:

1. This was the music for me—and it was *in* me.
2. I had stumbled upon something that resonated deeply with my core.

3. These were my people, and I was hopeful there would be more to meet.
4. This was a grassroots movement, fueled by fire, optimism, and creativity, still in its infancy but already rich in diversity.
5. All of this had been made possible by a press company called Beatwax, with whom I regularly connected from the *Warwick Boar* office. I realised then that cultivating genuine relationships was key—and I was lucky to learn that lesson before I turned 21.

At 20, my life began to dovetail with the Tribal intensity of the musicians and behind-the-scenes people I'd met at that particular Gathering.

CHAPTER THREE
WRITING THE WRONGS

I didn't realise it at the time, but 1993–1996 was essentially the training ground for everything that followed, mentally testing me on the road to steady, gainful employment in London.

After Tribal Gathering in 1995, I returned to campus eager to learn more about the dance music scene I had just experienced and the labels I had been reading about in Melody Maker and, to a lesser extent, in NME. The coverage in Melody Maker by two British journalists, Push and Ben Turner (with polite props to Sherman at The Controls), resonated with me more, especially since I had already seen the magazine take more serious steps to support electronic music, such as their Underworld cover the year before. As usual, I was making mental notes, but, like anyone experiencing something so pivotal at such an early age, I felt somewhat like a novice when it came to the history of house music. I needed a mentor, but that person hadn't materialised yet.

Back in '95, the major labels were starting to recognize the power of dance music, often with a sprinkling of piano and a cheap video featuring two or three semi-professional dancers. What was missing was the identity. Acts like Leftfield and Sunscreem (coincidentally both signed to Sony) were beginning to appear repeatedly on mixtapes and in club charts, but beyond the cognoscenti, it was difficult to find anyone who knew what the core members of these acts looked like. There was definitely something bubbling, but it was mostly on the commercial front. What was needed was something to tie all these elements together, to give the sound a proper visual and creative voice and direction.

As *Muzik* magazine's inaugural issue took hold of my subconscious, forever linked to the Tribal Gathering experience, I bought successive issues in the months that followed. I soaked up the quotes and listened to or recorded the Essential Mixes that helped me with my weekend house music homework. When my second year ended, I decided to stay in Leamington Spa for the summer, working at the high-street retail chain Woolworths and enjoying the relative peace and quiet of the Midlands.

In the summer of 1995, while Anna studied overseas in Siena for the year, I focused on my studies and immersed myself in local music activities. This included writing about club culture (I interviewed Paul Oakenfold on the phone during my second year, where he regaled me with stories of supermodels going through his record box) and hanging out with bands who came to campus. One of the bands I remember chatting with one Saturday night was Oui 3. Signed to MCA Records, they had just scored a hit in the UK with a song called *Break From The Old Routine*, but the three band members—Blair Booth, Philipp Erb, and Trevor Miles—seemed somewhat deflated by what was happening with their career. It wasn't their fault. Their cover of *For What It's Worth* by US rock band Buffalo Springfield had given them another hit, but their mishmash of looks and styles didn't fit into any specific box, which ultimately made them difficult to market for their major label bosses. I imagine that every major label hoped to sign another act as successful as Deee-Lite—but that was easier said than done, and there was only one Lady Miss Kier. The one major label act that smashed it in '93 and '94 with a series of undeniable singles and a platinum-selling album was The Stereo MCs, signed to Island Records.

The next time I checked in on Oui 3, the band had imploded. Interestingly, the British dance stars Faithless would later cite the band as an influence, but like One Dove, these acts couldn't continue with a second album on a major label without support from the top. Often, the major label's best idea of a "good idea" was simply to "make a cover version." Meanwhile, in my second year, I continued working hard, reading, revising, and doing enough to stay on top of things. I was determined to earn a 2:1.

Then, my third year came into focus in 1996. Aside from my studies, I was working on The Warwick Boar, hanging out with Anna (who would eventually become editor), and occasionally going to the movies. [1]

However, I think it's fair to say that my waking existence was mainly hotwired to learning about and understanding electronic music. I still politely listened to indie dance—and in the wake of Oasis, there was now more mid-range Britpop than you could shake a Shed Seven-shaped stick at—but it seemed that The Prodigy and The Chemical Brothers pointed the way to a far more exciting future than anything The Bluetones or new indie hopefuls like Cast could offer. Who recorded it, where it

---

1 David Fincher's *Seven* scar(r)ed us both to death but she was so petrified by the ending that we weren't allowed to sleep in the dark for a week.

was signed, where those acts were performing, and, in the case of anything on Creation, Deconstruction, or Heavenly Recordings, what was it that made these particular artists tick? I had to know these things. I was an impressionable boy scout based in Leamington Spa and saw myself as the (dance) music equivalent of the kid in *Almost Famous*, minus the backstage groupie controversy.

Some of those young, pioneering producers I met—One Dove, Sister Bliss from Faithless, Paul Oakenfold, BT, and The Orb among them—remain allies and friends today, and all of it can be traced back to my time at *The Warwick Boar* for three amazing years. Gig tickets, signed albums, and posters all remain in boxes, and if I didn't meet the artists (usually because other members of the Boar team wanted their thirty minutes with the famous), I'd ask for a signed poster for my third-year bedroom wall. [2]

Although I was serious about my degree (and I did get that 2:1), I was just too busy being twenty-one and soaking up everything the mid-nineties had to offer to care about politics or the trials and tribulations of Princess Diana. In my third year of studies, with Anna now back in the UK and in our new house, I experienced a year that was settled and calm, with just the occasional phone call home to my mum to check in. I was still very much enjoying the freedom that university represented. The road I lived on, Plymouth Place, looks exactly the same almost thirty years later. I guess not much changes in Leamington Spa.

If anything, my third year at university was the best year by far: I was living on a nice, quiet street near the station with Anna

---

[2] Here's looking at you, Dubstar and your naughty EMI debut album cover art for *Disgraceful*.

and a handful of carefully picked friends who all occasionally took turns doing the washing up. One of my flatmates, Chris Kirsch, was a designer of the inside pages of *The Boar*.[3] We had a nonchalant black cat living with us, and I had a nice view from my bedroom of the back garden. Most mornings, I'd wake up and watch *The Big Breakfast* on Channel 4 with Johnny Vaughan and Denise Van Outen. It seemed to sum up the spirit of the UK in a funny and light-hearted fashion and, sporadically, would feature faces from my childhood, like UK comedians Rik Mayall, and at the other end of the scale of success and humour, Keith Chegwin. But that was always part of its madcap charm. It was also an early home to future drag superstar Paul O'Grady, and I remember one of the most popular films of this era in the student house being the Australian movie caper *Priscilla, Queen of the Desert*. Remember, in the mid-90s, Australian soap operas and star power still had its grip on the UK— a hangover from the cultural force they had exerted on us from 1987 and 1988 onwards.

On Saturdays, after my shift behind the counter at Woolworths (better than McDonald's, but still pretty depressing to witness up close how many people wanted to buy singles by Boyzone), my favourite TV show was, naturally, *The X-Files*. But I do have one big memory of Woolworths beyond the Blur vs. Oasis media war. That was when the UK music industry got together to record the *Help* album, which, at times, felt like I had a secret hand in curating, even though I was only 21 and nowhere near it. There was one memorable photo of Noel Gallagher, Paul Weller,

---

[3] and we reconnected again recently: he is still with his partner Thorsten from all those years ago, and if that's not a heart-warming story, I don't know what is.

and Paul McCartney that fairly summed up the spirit of the charity project (they recorded a cover of *Come Together* as The Smokin' Mojo Filters). But as well as this Britpop supergroup, the record label War Child managed to get new and exclusive music and cover versions from Blur, Oasis, Suede, Massive Attack, Terry Hall, and Salad (a cute cover of *Dream a Little Dream*) and The Manic Street Preachers, whose cover of *Raindrops Keep Falling on My Head* was unusually sweet for them. It was also the first time that Radiohead unleashed *Lucky*, which has ultimately become one of the most loved records in their entire catalogue.

With free music arriving daily to *The Boar* (I can still remember the excitement of receiving brightly coloured promo club mixes on cassette from Cream), I was living the final year dream, frankly, and Leamington Spa remains a place I still visit every 18 months or so for a sneaky trip down memory lane. Every time I walk past the church, I hear the melody to The Verve's 'History' like clockwork. In truth, the market town has changed very little beyond the decimation of all the record stores I used to frequent. (Woolworths also closed for good across the country back in 2004, but I can still taste the pick 'n' mix sweets selection).[4]

Always loyal to acts I'd listened to early on, Oasis remained a favourite throughout these years, especially when *Wonderwall* broke the band globally but, wonderfully, missed the number one spot in the UK for its entire chart run. I was just so happy

---

[4] That said, if you're wondering what Leamington Spa looks like in colour, your best bet is to look at the cover of Ocean Colours Scene's nineties Britpop album *Moseley Shoals*: the memorial by which the band can be seen standing on is the Jephson Memorial in The Jephson Gardens and my third year house was just a hot step from that particular park.

to see a Creation band I liked go further than 18 Wheeler or The Boo Radleys (with no offence to either party). I still remember my well-intentioned concern for Creation when the CD single barcode on Oasis' *Roll With It* wouldn't bleep properly at the sales counter in Woolworths, unlike its neighbour in *Country House*. Like a good, loyal boy scout, I rang the *NME* News Desk to tell them the news, and they printed the barcode story the following week, as they would about absolutely anything noteworthy or otherwise involving Noel, Liam, or Oasis in general. (I'd wager that it lost them a few hundred sales, but the fact *Country House* was considerably cheaper to purchase that first week was the major factor that caused it to sell like hot cakes.)

Looking back, it's clear that everything that happened required thought, paper, and ink to turn it from fax to fact. So when it came to magazines, I would buy as many as my weekly wage would allow, which was quite a lot. Trips to the library were important, but so were trips to venues from London to Birmingham and back. I was an indie kid with a fascination for the slowly fermenting electronic music scene and have amazing memories of bands and shows I got to experience thanks to PR companies like the sadly-departed White Noise and Beatwax, who sent me Annie Nightingale's now-seminal *Annie On One* compilation on vinyl. A record so well thought out and beautifully curated, it still remains a source of inspiration, as well as a near-perfect time capsule.

Put together by Heavenly and Annie in tandem, her wish list of tracks fairly summed up the spirit of 1996 at the edges of clubland as described in *Melody Maker* and in the pages of *Muzik*. Sabres Of Paradise - *Theme* opens the first side, and it's the full seven-minute version. Then there's *The Age Of Love* by

Jam and Spoon, a record that would later find a new home on Ibiza's Space Terrace, courtesy of a young David Guetta. Then there's Dreadzone's mix of *Lookee Here* by Transglobal Underground, before Kris Needs gives Primal Scream's recent return single *Rocks* a new lick of paint over on side two. Just before side two comes to an end, *Da Funk* by a new French act called Daft Punk makes an early compilation appearance. Annie was a dance music tastemaker through and through, and bearing in mind that even in 1996 she would have been seen as an elder in the community, it's incredible that she had another twenty-five years of active radio service after this came out. Side three and four were equally sublime, with side four returning to Weatherall with his mix of Black Sheep and then Flowered Up's *Weekender* to close, all twelve minutes and fifty-six seconds of flower power.

"Tune in every Saturday night/Sunday morning for The Chill Out Zone," said the note on the back of the sleeve. "2 'til 4AM, Radio One 97-99FM. Stay up!"

I still think the green cover image of Annie on that compilation is a classic.

But beyond *The Chill Out Zone*, there was still indie music to explore in '96. So, we'd travel to Birmingham to meet a band like Belly, hang backstage with plucky new acts like Ash, Sleeper, and The Longpigs, or I'd informally chat with Sister Bliss from Faithless after she'd visited Warwick to DJ at— ahem!— Rolf's Bar one Saturday night. I remember seeing her set one Saturday night, full of future anthems on the increasingly successful Cheeky Records imprint, and one in particular called *Insomnia* that had something about it. I'd also seen her name on records as a creator in the band Faithless, who were really just coming

CHAPTER THREE: WRITING THE WRONGS

together themselves in 1995 and 1996. *Salva Mea* was their first release in July 1995, and it was the first single from their debut album *Reverence*, which would later become a global smash, thanks in (most) part to *Insomnia*. But there was something about this band of brothers and sister(s), which featured not only a female producer and keyboard player but also a behind-the-scenes producer I liked called Rollo and a Buddhist frontman called Maxi Jazz. *Salva Mea* featured backing vocals from Rollo's sister and future megastar Dido, but back in 1995, she was merely credited on the back rather than the front sleeve. Like INXS and Suede, Faithless appealed to me because the music was cool and clever, and the band's image was a long way from pedestrian. It wouldn't be long before they would be playing at The Jazz Cafe in Camden, along with another founder member called Jamie Catto, who sang on their next single, *Don't Leave*. After playing at Warwick, the classically trained keyboard player Sister Bliss rang me back the week after (at home, I remember the call!) to chat further. What a legend, and a genuinely lovely lady with a unique, never-to-be-repeated perspective.

That's not quite the same thing you'd say about Rolf Harris in 2024. Invited (ironically) to Warwick back in '91 to open a bar named after him, dusty Rolf was so chuffed that he gave the students' union one of his paintings, presumably unaware that he'd been picked as a joke because he was so unfashionable at the time. He'd have much, much bigger—and self-created—problems towards the end of his life, as any Kate Bush fan will be able to tell you. I also became friends at this point with Mick and Keith fanatic and Annie Nightingale favourite Kris Needs, who'd lived in Aylesbury and would occasionally come to Warwick Uni to DJ.

He would regale us with stories about U2, Primal Scream, and The Rolling Stones, and once again, this seemed like a world worth exploring after we'd finished drinking our pints of lager in search of the next tall tale. He was what we now call a True Believer, and thirty years later, he is still leading the same life today at 70 and writing the occasional music missive for *Mojo* from his new home in Suffolk. Looking back, he was perhaps the first person to not only open a door but also actually pull me through it.[5]

Looking back at all of this from the vantage point of 2024, and in terms of pure profitability, it's hard not to view this time as a formative yet golden era of dance music and the intertwined indie/electronic print press. 1994 saw acts like D:Ream reach number one (for four weeks!), and Pete Tong's *Essential Selection* and EMI's chart-chomping, platinum-selling Positiva label, in particular, seemed to predict the American house hits months before they duly hit the UK Top Ten. Tunes like *Everybody Needs Somebody* by Ruffneck, major UK hits from Reel 2 Reel, Judy Cheeks, and the most handbag act in the pack, Manchester's M People, who scored hit after hit after first breaking through with a cover of *Someday* and Sasha's timeless remix of *How Can I Love You More*.[6]

It was always exciting witnessing acts gain momentum from the ground up, and beyond Oasis, these acts included Leftfield,

---

5 Pleasingly, we would meet again at The Manumission Motel on the roof in '99. Circles, circles, and circles again.

6 (M People were signed to BMG/Deconstruction, for all the pedants out there who care about detail but Deconstruction, with their love of proper N-Joi-esque rave was my favourite mainstream dance label that wasn't Perfecto.)

CHAPTER THREE: WRITING THE WRONGS

Moloko, Washington DC's Brian 'BT' Transeau and his teenage buddies, and brothers in electronic arms, Ali Shirazinia and Sharam Tayebi, AKA Deep Dish. I first met the Maryland-born child prodigy/producer and future *Muzik* magazine cover star, Brian Transeau, backstage in Brighton at a night called Babealicious, thanks to his Perfecto press officer at East West, Shane O'Neill. BT, in particular, had something that, in later years, would almost become a defining characteristic for dance acts trying to break through the multiverse of social media: charisma. Transeau had musical talent in spades, as well as endless anecdotes about Justin Timberlake, Britney Spears, and his childhood fascination with all things new wave. He would casually toss things out like: "My monitor was broken, but the incredible Stewart Copeland was kind enough to give me The Police's touring Fairlight monitor." (Side note: this is an *actual quote* from Brian at the time.)

As much as I loved them, this was a very different world from the one presented in the UK by Tall Paul and the UK-centric Turnmills crew. Chopin, Debussy, and Rachmaninoff were BT's early guiding lights. As a child, his hands weren't yet large enough to play the 19th-century Steinway grand piano he'd inherited from his grandmother, so Brian's parents bought him a toy keyboard on which he would try to reproduce the latest pop hits. By the age of seven, he was formally studying classical music at the Washington Conservatoire. Clearly, there were many reasons why we could become good friends. I remember being slightly perplexed when he produced *NSYNC's* staccato single *Pop* (where he even referenced himself at the start of the song!), but ultimately, he was soon forgiven.

Anna and I made one more trip that shot a hole through my head. We were invited to The Que Club to see an early all-night Essential Selection in Birmingham, which featured some of the biggest names in global dance. Pete was joined by Paul Oakenfold, Sasha, Danny Rampling, and Billy Ray Martin, who had only just escaped from Electribe 101 but had yet to score a hit with *Your Loving Arms*. BT's music was all over the five-hour club production – he was the hottest producer on the progressive planet. While Paul Oakenfold signed him, Sasha remixed him, and Pete, not to be outdone, got him to remix his baby acts on London Records, where he ran the ship during the week. He's a more trance-leaning proposition these days, but his single with Sasha, *Ride*, remains one of the best acid productions of its time, and, as Sasha later told me proudly, it was hammered by Andrew Weatherall in his prime (and yes, "prime" is relative, but in 1998, Weatherall most definitely was).

After three years, I got my all-important English degree before coming back to earth with a bang when that elusive first step on the career ladder proved impossible to grasp in '96. Friends were taking jobs in the city in accounting or with – shudder – boring local businesses, but I decided to take a job earning £122 a week in my friend Steve's record shop, Round Sounds, instead. I was back living at home after an incredible three years of busy campus life, and while Anna and I still soldiered on with one year left of her 4 year Italian degree, it wasn't ideal. Much later, in adult life, I asked Mum what she thought of me working in a record store for the best part of two years. She was pretty blunt: "I was horrified, dear." I've still never worn a proper work suit outside of a wedding or a funeral.

CHAPTER THREE: WRITING THE WRONGS

Despite having no real road map, music journalism was still the only logical step for me after Warwick. I would voraciously read the print press every week for their electronic coverage, and I was aching to bring my own stamp of authority to proceedings in the right place. I still had no desire to take a corporate route, but I didn't think I was cool or clued up enough about electronic music to go straight to *Muzik* magazine (I was just too shy for my own good sometimes), so I tried my luck writing for *The Times* and especially at the *NME* – another IPC publication – first. Having spoken on the phone a few times from my third-year house, the full-time News Editor, Mat Smith (if you've seen *Almost Famous*, essentially the *NME* version of Rolling Stone's Ben Fong-Torres), was super supportive, and to my delight, he soon got me interviewing artists from Krist Novoselic of Nirvana to Ash. Over on the *NME* 'Vibes' desk, their dance section, I was soon interviewing people like Goldie (around his second record, the Bowie-featuring double album *Saturnz Return*) for full-page features.

But I didn't share the steely *Vibes* Editor Ben Wilmott's fascination for abrasive jungle artists like Ed Rush and Optical, and my taste was way too pop to fully immerse myself in all things Aphex, Rephlex, or R&S. So I would write about Skint or Wall of Sound acts like The Propellerheads or Les Rythmes Digitales, whose pop culture reference points – Shannon, David Bowie, Shirley Bassey, and James Bond – seemed much more in tune with my own internal audio.

The rest of the *NME*'s team? Honestly – and I really don't mind saying this as most of them are no longer in the business of writing – not that friendly or supportive. Some of the faces and names whose work I would see again and again in print –

step forward Steve Sutherland, Ted Kessler, Johnny Cigarettes – all worked very hard behind the scenes, and I remember saying hello to Dele Fadele (R.I.P.) and being greeted with a distrustful scowl. But beyond a very occasionally vocally supportive Johnny Cigarettes, arguably their most talented writer to my mind, *NME* really didn't feel like my editorial gang. When I told the live desk I liked cheerfully ramshackle indie act Gomez, I was greeted with an expression that said: "Thanks, but please don't darken the live desk door ever again." On that occasion, I had picked a band who didn't fit the internal credentials, possibly because they had more in common with *NME*'s rivals over at *MM* – but in 1997 and 1998, I was still finding my feet and my taste in the world of music, and I certainly hadn't been to enough events to feel at home in the underground dance community. So I would return to my job at Round Sounds in Burgess Hill with a head full of dreams but only £40 in occasional writing fees to show for it. These small, sporadic payments weren't enough to fuel a career as a journalist or justify the major move to London.

And then, one afternoon after visiting *NME*, I took it upon myself to make an impromptu visit to the *Muzik* magazine office before heading home to Burgess Hill. Beyond my 18 hours with Russell at Tribal Gathering, it was by far the smartest decision I made that side of the year 2000. Most people would call, mail, or – best of all – fax (and boy, did they love faxing their DJ charts), but very few were conversing on mobiles, and your main question to the web was via Ask Jeeves.

I distinctly remember walking in and feeling a different energy from the one I'd experienced at *NME* and *Melody Maker*. I was

22 and eager to learn, and I immediately cornered the confident reviews editor Calvin Bush, a bespectacled Scot with bags of character and a fellow word pedant, who pretty much on the spot commissioned me to write about electronic albums in 1998 and early 1999. Between reviews of new albums by Faithless or Fatboy Slim, I'd occasionally be asked to pitch and hopefully write reviews of other acts I loved. *Muzik*'s Ben Turner – an evangelistic, excitable electronic music believer from Oxford who understood the mechanics of dance music better than almost any music journalist in the industry – sailed the ship from the very beginning, with Push, a kind-hearted music journalist from Brentford whose real name is Christopher Dawes. An early assignment for *Muzik* sent me to Bournemouth to review a club night featuring LTJ Bukem, and after the gig, Bukem dropped me off in Blackfriars from the tour bus, where I submitted the copy at 7 a.m. and then got the train to the shire in time for the shop opening at 9 a.m. The excitement of being inside Bukem's futuristic tour bus for two hours alone was enough to make me want more. When Massive Attack played at The Brighton Centre, I reviewed their show for *Muzik* and semi-predicted the departure of the band's DJ Mushroom in my review. I still love Massive Attack with the same intensity today.

Alongside Calvin, the office was a who's who of hip London scenesters, including an extremely outgoing young DJ and party-starter called Rob da Bank, an unashamed hippy from Portsmouth whose real name was Robert Gorham, and a house music fanatic in the form of the always well-turned-out feature editor Frank Tope, who'd come over from *Mixmag* and who had an encyclopaedic knowledge of music that I admired immensely.

Ben Turner was *Muzik*'s main 'music' editor and always seemed to be jetting off somewhere exotic, like Ibiza, Detroit, or Singapore, in search of adventure. The young editorial assistant and later clubs editor, Karen Young, a fashion-conscious elfin brunette who left behind a role in record company land to join the *Muzik* team and took no nonsense from the boys, completed the initial quartet. We'd later all become fast friends, mixing business and pleasure like our lives depended on it.

I recently watched a documentary about XFM with Stephen Merchant and Ricky Gervais, and the similarities really struck me: we both had structure, but there was an awful lot of activity that involved trying to get ideas and interviews off the ground with one or two proper grown-ups in the room trying to ensure that the wheels weren't sheared off. But while XFM was an alternative radio station, *Muzik* was an IPC-owned proposition that had to put out a monthly magazine of quality and note, with a lot more attention to detail and, crucially, a much stronger sense of permanence: once the magazine had gone to press, there was no going back, which was equal parts frightening and exhilarating.

This was, it transpired, my community after all. And after completing a few early missions for *Muzik* (including my first cover feature with Sheffield's Gatecrasher Kids – which paid £600 thanks to the unusually long word count, an absolute win for 24-year-old me), I felt safe and at home in a world I had previously only observed from the periphery. The first artist I ever interviewed for *Muzik* was French disco producer and future pop star Bob Sinclar, talking about his new record and the "few loops" he'd made together with Daft Punk's Thomas Bangalter. The song was called *Gym Tonic*, and it sampled Jane Fonda's famous 1980s workout video. It was – and still is – a serious jam. I still remember where I was when I did that interview: it was upstairs in the office of my friend Steve's record store, Round Sounds, and while it wasn't the most exciting interview I ever submitted, I saw and heard the record become a Space Terrace anthem via various hype and DJ charts.

All of a sudden, indie landfill like Hurricane #1 and a creatively waning Oasis couldn't compete with an emerging Daft Punk, the smell of Air, the returning Chemical Brothers, and the eventual lure of Ibiza, which, in reality, was much, much closer than I could have dreamed of.

CHAPTER FOUR
MAKING MOVES

Thanks to a smart career-shifting suggestion from my Islington-based sister, Elena (who by now had three children—Cherelle, Antonella, and Hayden), and the sudden availability of my sister-in-law Mary's spacious ground-floor flat in Leyton, East London, by April 1999, I'd made the big life leap from woozy West Sussex to the edgy and ultimately more exciting East London. I was paying £400 in rent to my sister-in-law and made that then-significant chunk of change work with a mixture of electronic writing assignments for *Muzik*, *The Times*, *NME* (their underground dance music section, *Vibes*, was still fairly strong in '99, mainly because the burgeoning dance scene in the capital and around the country was so vibrant and exciting), and a modest but cool website called Music 365. There, a kind and excellent hip-hop scribe named Angus Batey gave me regular work and, more importantly, made me feel welcome whenever I visited him for a coffee.

Looking back, I had no choice but to switch things up and make the change work to my advantage: there was no going back to the shire. If there was a suitably cool party line-up, I'd pop in for an hour or two, and if there was a bigger rave in town (I always called central London "town") worth investigating, I'd head in with one of my friends and crawl home to Leyton in the morning.

Aside from the sleeker techno sounds at The End, the biggest sound of this era in London and Brighton was the bouncy, brash "big beat" phenomenon. This is where I realised again that talking to press officers was invaluable. People like Ruth Drake and Ed Cartwright were royally plugged into the dance music mainline via their clients: Skint and Wall of Sound as independent labels, Basement Jaxx and Fatboy Slim as artists, and Brighton, Brixton, and Farringdon as specific rave hubs we would all return to again and again.

Given that I was born in Brighton, it still felt like a home away from home when I went back for the odd jaunt to The Hobgoblin Pub, The Concorde, or, before that, a funny little scout hut where Fatboy Slim's career as a DJ and producer was properly incubated.[1]

"At that point, the Social and the Boutique were the focal points for what had become a movement," says Cook when we speak. "In those days, dance compilations used to outsell artist albums!"

My favourite memory of this era was definitely at The Hobgoblin Pub, which is still standing loud and proud in 2024 (and now calls itself "Brighton's Best Student Pub & Beer Garden"). Back in 1998 and '99, however, it was the best place for a scrape or an after-party—provided you had the right invite. Around 1998, Fatboy Slim had just started bubbling through as a pop star, so

---

[1] *On the Floor at the Boutique* is a must-hear for anyone who wants to dig deeper on the subject.

CHAPTER FOUR: MAKING MOVES

seeing Norman Cook up close and personal was an opportunity too good to miss. I vividly remember his secret weapon at the party: a bootleg of *Rockafella Skank* mixed with *Satisfaction* by The Rolling Stones, soon to be known as *Satisfaction Skank*. The two records fit together like hand in glove.

The atmosphere was pure carnage, partly thanks to Mike and Claire Manumission, who were in attendance. For 23-year-old me, this felt like the most fun I could possibly be having—all while proudly sporting what I'll call my "big beat starter pack." [2]

Once I was firmly settled into Leyton life (essential items: a new white Apple Mac, a landline, two tax-deductible Technics 1210 decks, a mixer and speakers, and a weekly visit to Oxford Street to check out the latest vinyl releases), things began to click. I remember all the records I bought during this era because they helped shape and define me. Early singles like Destiny's Child's *Bills, Bills, Bills*, Sasha's peerless and timeless *Xpander* EP, and Fatboy Slim's *Better Living Through Chemistry* LP all made their way back to the house by the park—and often earned me the wrath of the neighbours upstairs when Beyoncé's voice got too loud after 8 p.m. Which, admittedly, was often.

I littered my bedroom with hundreds of records, extensions of my identity—because that's exactly what they were. I had a garden in Leyton too, but gardening wasn't high on the agenda in 1999 or 2000.

Various other things happened that summer. Eventually, *NME* told me my regular writing services were no longer required (what

---

2 Meaning a red Jacques Lu Cont band t-shirt that said "Jacques Up!" on it, my none-more-All Saints baggy trousers and trusty blue spectacles.

a relief! My enthusiasm for their platform had already been derailed by their lacklustre demeanour). Fortunately, *Music 365* helped pay the rent by commissioning longer features where I felt comfortable expressing my still-developing opinions—and, crucially, paying by the word. A special shout-out is also due to Paul Conroy at *The Times* and his heir apparent, Ed Potton, who not only commissioned a two-page Underworld feature but also had me review albums for the Saturday pullout. In short, I made it through 1999 by writing about quality pop and cutting-edge electronic dance music, while catching up with new and old friends alike.

Now the manager of Detroit-born techno DJ and raconteur Seth Troxler and UK lynchpin Damian Lazarus, former Darling Department MD Ed Cartwright was instrumental in bringing key acts to the main dance music magazines. Back then, he was a canny operator with a crack team of young staff whose taste often mirrored my own. If the Darling Department sent me the new single by Leftfield (in '99, that would have been *Phat Planet*), The Propellerheads (*Dive!*), or The Wiseguys (*Ooh La La*), I wanted to dig deeper. When *Ooh La La* ended up as the soundtrack for a Budweiser ad with a singing frog, it felt like club culture was bumping up against the mainstream again—a phenomenon reminiscent of David Rodigan on Capital Radio or Pete Tong's early days at the same station, when they were helping incubate future hits by the likes of Faithless and Underworld. In other words, I began to pay attention to tastemakers whose roles in radio and press helped bring their favourite artists to wider audiences.

Ed and his Darling Department partner Dan had now taken over the company from its founder, Marion, and together they assembled a brilliant team of press officers. This team would go on to work with acts including The Killers, Hard-Fi, Tom Vek, and one of my favourite Scottish synth-pop stars, Mr. *Drop the Pressure* himself—Mylo.[3]

The best thing about leaving *NME* was that just a one-minute walk from the main IPC Tower lay the place that would change my life, my bank balance, and most importantly, my dance music perspective. Situated on the first floor of Hatfield House on Stamford Street, even as a freelancer, the *Muzik* magazine office increasingly felt like the hub where my electronic worldview was being shaped. It was, essentially, an incubator where editorial decisions shaped careers and elevated DJs' iconography to new heights. It was curation on a level—and of a quality—that *Mixmag* and *DJ* simply couldn't match.

Before I joined, I saw this happen month after month with producers like the BBC Radio 1 production and presenter favourite Tall Paul, the grumpy but brilliant baron of techno Dave Clarke, and an early cover featuring Camden-based Faithless, fresh off their performance at The Jazz Café with Maxi Jazz. Unlike *NME* and *Melody Maker*, *Muzik* wasn't as hung up on race, so while women didn't grace the cover often between 1995 and 1999, Black drum 'n' bass legends like Goldie and Roni Size were regular features. One cover I frequently revisit is the

---

3 Indeed, all of the people who played their part behind the scenes are still working hard in the digital age, whether that's Tom March who is - deep breath, because this is a lot - now Chairman and CEO of the Capitol Music Group in LA but back then, he would always send me records by Tiga or Mylo with a cute hand-written note. I've said it before and I will no doubt say it again: the personal touch always goes further.

issue centred around Stardust's *Music Sounds Better With You*. We were always quick off the mark, and Daft Punk's Thomas Bangalter, still in his early twenties, regularly appeared in the magazine.

The design team was led by the tall, debonair, and ever-stylish Declan Fahy, who was either working on potential covers or pulling together features with the help of *Muzik*'s chief sub editor, Tom Mugridge. Tom was a friendly, whip-smart but undeniably countercultural figure whose musical sensibilities were evident when he interviewed Andrew Weatherall alongside Throbbing Gristle for a feature. Ben had his own office—where all manner of conversations could take place away from prying ears—and, in my corner, you had myself, Frank, Rob da Bank, and eventually Karen Young.

To set the scene for those who missed out on 1990s magazine publishing, the office was, in short, chaos. CDs arrived by the dozen with press releases in brown jiffy bags every single day. Vinyl shipments came packed with even more press releases, and at the bottom of each was a phone number for Virgin's Dance Department, Slice PR, or someone at Zzonked. These were scattered across desks along with empty coffee cups and snack packets. This was also the era of free promotional T-shirts, and British clubbing institutions like Soma, Junior Boy's Own, or Skint kept our undernourished torsos covered for years.

Much like a daily post office lottery, some of the records we received were stone-cold classics. Some albums arrived with sweets, a few Daft Punk double-packs—now worth more than a good month's rent—found their way into the mix, and some of the world's best remix talent took major label dollars to rework

CHAPTER FOUR: MAKING MOVES

tracks by Dido, Britney Spears, or The Rolling Stones.[4] Before I had my own desk at *Muzik*, many of these mailers landed daily at my door in Leyton. The best of them are now safely in my collection, alongside press releases from people who would go on to become future managers, scenesters and major label presidents.

While my former *Warwick Boar* alumnus Stephen Merchant had quickly secured a role at the BBC (I remember visiting him around '98 and feeling exceedingly jealous that he'd already found his groove), my confidence grew with each major writing assignment—even if I cringe a bit now at some of what I wrote back then. Looking back, there are occasional flashes of my voice coming through, but much of it was just a tangled mess of overwrought phrasing. That began to change when I interviewed Deep Dish in Miami.[5]

By then, I had been at *Muzik* for a year. The night before the interview, I had stayed up dancing to Danny Tenaglia at Space until dawn. I did what any sleep-deprived 25-year-old would do in the same situation: I crawled back to my hotel around 10 a.m., grabbed three hours of sleep (at most), took the hottest shower of my life, and made my way to a sushi lunch at 1 p.m. with Ali and Sharam of Deep Dish at the impossibly fancy, five-star Delano Hotel on South Beach. Despite my fatigue, I listened intently as the duo riffed off each other for an hour. The resulting two-page piece turned out really well—mainly because, by that point, I had developed a balance of curiosity and attentiveness. Robby's

---

[4] Yes, we are specifically looking at Washington DC house duo Deep Dish and the chart-straddling pop-house hero Armand Van Helden here.

[5] (and I should also give a shout out to Rob da Bank whose kind email about my Ali and Sharam feature has always stayed with me)

email congratulating me on my writing was the cherry on top, the kind of boost every young writer needs.

As I approached my mid-twenties and the prospect of full-time employment, one thing became clear: what I cared about most—consistently and instinctively—was where electronic music was heading, my friends and family, and finding a job in an environment where I could balance all these priorities without the constant worry of mounting bills at the end of each month. My only option was to keep chipping away as a determined freelancer and hope I wouldn't end up being dismissed as too junior to be taken seriously.

There was one final hurdle to cross before my career truly took off. Shortly after I moved to London, Ben Turner called to ask if I'd be interested in flying to Ibiza to write for *The Islander*, a magazine co-produced with the mischievous IPC crew behind *Loaded Magazine*. The offer was incredible: flights and hotels covered by IPC (!), an expense account, and a salary of £400 a week. My task was to submit club reviews, interview promoters, grill bleary-eyed clubbers on the beach at Bora Bora, and chat with industry heavyweights like Judge Jules, Pete Tong, or Dave Pearce—whether after their sets or back in the UK. Honestly, at 24 years old, I would have done it for free.

That summer, I ended up visiting Ibiza six times. On one of those trips, I was sent to cover (or cover up for) Rob da Bank, who had disappeared for several days after an epic Monday night/Tuesday morning session at Manumission.[6]

---

[6] That club had a lot to answer for and there's a very funny Rob da Bank Muzik print feature that discusses making Ibiza work on a budget, which RDB was

CHAPTER FOUR: MAKING MOVES

Wait, you want to hear about Manumission? Let's start by saying that if you were really pushing Ibiza to its limits, you'd "Do The Triple." This meant starting at Space on a Sunday, ideally by lunchtime; heading to DC10 for Circo Loco early Monday morning (hence the phrase "Monday morning session" on their 2000-era promo material); and finally ending up at Manumission on Monday night at Privilege. This 10,000-capacity megadome, located in the middle of the island but closer to the British enclave of San Antonio, was the crown jewel of Ibiza's party scene.

The smart move was to arrive around 1 a.m.—guest lists closed at 2 a.m., but the real action didn't begin until 3 a.m. Packed with wide-eyed Brits and Europeans, Manumission in '99 (and for a few years afterwards) was both the island's most successful and controversial party. While Mike Manumission was the face of it all, his brother Andy worked behind the scenes alongside Mike's then-wife Claire and Andy's wife, Dawn. Two couples, each playing distinct roles in a chaotic but mesmerising production. It felt like a wild stage play—not unlike the ones I'd seen in school, but with more debauchery than West Sussex could ever dream of. The soundtrack was a boozy, hedonistic mix of house and techno, keeping the crowd moving until sunrise.

The music didn't have the smooth, refined vibe of Renaissance or Yoshitoshi nights at Pacha, but the real draw was the spectacle: trapeze artists soaring above, jaw-dropping stage performances, and a feeling of unrestrained freedom. Missing Privilege—or

---

duly made Balearic guinea pig for. Essentially, he was doing it the Worker's Way; those days are long gone.

its infamous after-party spot, The Manumission Motel—meant you'd missed out on a quintessential Ibiza experience.

I still have a handful of blurry Snappy Snaps photos I took at 8 a.m., trying to capture the surreal scene of watching the sunrise over Ibiza Town through Privilege's massive glass windows. The elation of surviving until the end of the night, as the final tracks played, was unmatched.

While I adored hearing my favourite players at Pacha (Deep Dish, Masters At Work, the list goes on), going to Manumission felt like attending the cup final. The music was powered by big beat, 80s Balearic classics, and Carl Cox-style techno-trance in equal measures. It was home to legends like Alfredo, Fatboy Slim (in his peak-madness era, when he first met Zoe Ball), and a friendly resident DJ named Griff, who occasionally got well-deserved features in *Muzik*.

Of course, the weekly onstage antics of Mike and Claire were infamous, a focal point beyond the acrobatics above. Manumission was where you'd spot genuine pop icons, legendary athletes, and sometimes both in one—like Diego Maradona, a larger-than-life figure in every sense.

I often found myself in the big beat-flavoured side room, which had a fantastic view of the sunrise. DJs like Jon Carter (Monkey Mafia head honcho and often Norman Cook's 90s sparring partner) and his West London rival, the always-spirited Derek Dahlarge, were frequent fixtures. Alfredo always seemed to show up at just the right time with the perfect track, adding a touch of magic to the mix.

When the sun came up, it marked a pivotal moment. And since the club wasn't far from the main road, it was usually easy to find a free taxi around 8 a.m. to head to the next destination. For me, that was often The Mezzanine Bar near my hotel—or, if we were really pushing it, The Manumission Motel, where a more intimate after-party would be underway.

The best part? Some of these partygoers were becoming genuine friends: Norman Cook and his then-girlfriend Zoe Ball, occasional members of Primal Scream, the producer I'd met at Warwick, Kris Needs (the Stones-obsessed leader of Secret Knowledge), Carl Cox with his loyal tour manager Garrie Barnes (R.I.P.), and even the irreverent Scottish author Irvine Welsh, now famous for *Trainspotting*.

These were characters in the story of my life, etched into my internal book. Sometimes, looking back, I still wonder if certain things really happened. Occasionally, I'll ask someone from that era, "Did this actually happen?" The answer is almost always the same: *"Yes."*

Originally opened in 1998, the Manumission Motel exuded a sense of naughtiness even from the outside—so you can only imagine the scenes behind its closed doors. It was always a 24- to 36-hour whirlwind, which explains why Tuesday nights on the island have traditionally been quiet. Even the most committed hedonists need a breather before Wednesday's festivities, especially when Subliminal at Pacha became the midweek epicenter of Ibiza Town partying.

Manumission was also the first party to bring Fatboy Slim to the island, and being a collector, I still have a handful of flyers from that summer tucked into a scrapbook—whether I actually attended those parties or not. The flyers themselves were an iconic element of their marketing, but the Coco Loco bar, with its drag queens and unapologetic glam, was where the real drama and color came alive. While much has been said about the infamous sex shows, to me, that was just one small part of the story. Entering Manumission felt like stepping into a surreal, cinematic world, and leaving before dawn—before the night's chaos had fully played out—was simply unthinkable.

One flyer I dug out recently captures the spirit of that time perfectly, complete with weekly updates from the much-missed writer and Motel regular, Howard Marks.

"Monday nights at Privilege – 5,000 PTS with this manuscript, 6,000 without. Tuesday morning 'CARRY-ON' at Space – 3,000 PTS with this manuscript, 4,000 PTS without. Cheapest form of entry is with this Manumission flyer. Manumission Millennium in Ibiza: info 0044 (0) 7000 462686.

'Come and crown Victoria, Queen Bee of the Pox Britannica.'"

My ever-stylish friend Nigel, who I first met outside The Mezzanine Bar in Ibiza Town, summed it up best. "When you arrived, you were fresh meat," he said of our early island encounters. "But now, you're seasoned brisket." (Or was it biscuit? The exact phrase hardly matters.)

I can still picture my 1999 Ibiza outfit: grey, box-fresh Nike trainers bought during a mall visit with Underworld in the U.S.; light grey slacks versatile enough for day or night, impervious to rain or stains; and a trusty black man bag to carry my phone (a necessity, as I had a tendency to leave things behind). Miraculously, I never lost a single thing that summer—except perhaps my sanity at Manumission.

Musically, 1999 felt like a hangover from 1998, which had peaked with Bob Sinclar's *Gym Tonic* and its unforgettable Jane

Fonda workout sample. I'd been desperate to visit Ibiza in '98, but my travels that year only extended to Gran Canaria with Russell—a trip that we did on a budget and involved little in the way of gyms or tonics.

1999, however, was all about *Big Love* by Pete Heller, Paul Van Dyk's trance anthem *Binary Finary* (trance was massive that summer), and *King of My Castle* by Chris Brann's Wamdue Project. Back then, I hadn't yet become the club snob I (regrettably) am today. So, my nights were spent hopping from Pacha—where house heavyweights like Deep Dish and Erick Morillo reigned supreme—to Space on Sundays, losing myself to sets from Cassius, Carl Cox, and Steve Lawler on the terrace. And, of course, Tuesday mornings were for Manumission, dancing to Alfredo and friends as the sun rose.

One standout memory from that summer is a house bootleg that sampled Michael Jackson's disco classic *Off the Wall*. Alfredo played it relentlessly, and I heard it just about everywhere I went. That track became the unofficial anthem of the season, a constant reminder of an unforgettable summer.[7]

As well as Roger Sanchez, we featured Fatboy Slim on the cover of one issue of *The Islander*. The Darling Department PR team arranged for me to meet Norman at his palatial beachside home in Hove. This was peak Slim in the UK—his recent *You've Come a Long Way, Baby* was a multi-platinum success—

---

[7] For the nugget diggers out there, it's a French house cut and I heard Daft Punk play it at a half-empty El Divino one Thursday too. It was called *Tonite* by Deaf N Dumb Crew and I even thanked Thomas and Guy for playing it when they finished their set! They were very, very sweet about it and it's a memory I cherish.)

so, frankly, I was living the dream. There I was, chatting with a 1990s hero about music, DJ culture, and his impending marriage to Zoe Ball, whom he had met and serenaded in Ibiza. Was there anything Love Island couldn't do for the true believers of that era? The magic was everywhere, and I couldn't wait for Ben to call me again, asking me to return to Ibiza. It became so easy to get there from London that it started to feel as casual as catching a train to Brighton—just an hour longer. In many ways, this ease is why Ibiza has always appealed to Brits: a two-hour flight, a quick wave of the passport at customs, and *boom*! You're back on the world's undisputed number-one party island. Is it any wonder I always came home half a stone lighter after a week on the White Isle?

But let's pause and dig deeper for a moment.

Getting close to artists brings its own set of dilemmas. I've never wanted to betray an artist's confidence; that's simply not the kind of journalist I ever wanted to be. It also doesn't align with how I've always viewed electronic music—first and foremost as a community, rather than just an industry. However, anyone who thinks today's much-maligned "clickbait journalism" is a new phenomenon should be aware of its analogue predecessor: the "killer pull quote."

To put it bluntly (and perhaps a little crassly), a killer pull quote—a controversial, often out-of-context one-liner from the interview—helped shift magazines off shelves. It was often the primary reason a casual reader would pick up a publication. This led to sensationalism and, all too often, recriminations. The better the pull quote, the more likely you were to land your next major assignment. It didn't always win friends among PR teams, inner circles, or the artists themselves, but the 1990s mentality was predominantly "Us vs. Them." Music journalism back then was far less collaborative than it is today, in part due to the rise of social media culture and declining print sales.

In the mid-90s, if a DJ criticised a club or a fellow selector, the magazine would plaster that quote on the cover. Take *Muzik*'s infamous "Hang the DJ" back page, where Ben Turner would call out an artist for something outrageous—often "selling out." For instance, British proto-superstar DJ Jeremy Healy found himself skewered for quips like, "I don't like New Age Travelers; I don't walk around with a shovel myself!"

There's no doubt about what the team—and, above them, the suits demanding sales—wanted: a dynamite interview packed with quotable lines that could spark conversation (and, ideally, increase magazine sales). The cover image was important too—*Muzik* had at least a dozen covers, from The Chemical Brothers to Eminem, Sasha, and Carl Cox, that still hold up today. But it was the sound of an artist letting loose that elevated a feature from pedestrian to peak-time.

I rarely used quotes that would cause serious friction, though I distinctly remember Bora Bora beach DJ Gee being irate over my description of "his" beach in 2000. For the most part, I realised life was too short to burn bridges with a DJ who had explicitly requested that a particular quote not be used. It just wasn't worth it.

It's not hard to see why artists have grown wary of these kinds of features. Sure, it was fun for the magazine to sell a few hundred extra copies with a headline that tapped into readers' own secret frustrations. But those same headlines often left PR teams cowering in fear of irate managers. Here are three particularly incendiary *Muzik* cover lines that caused their fair share of fallout:

- Karl Hyde: "I am an alcoholic." (*March 1999*)
- Armand Van Helden: "Fuck the British powers that be!" (*May 2000*)
- Adam Freeland: "I challenge Oakenfold to mix two breakbeat records." (*November 2001*)

These kinds of statements could cause chaos. After the Adam Freeland issue, the Brighton-based breakbeat DJ told me he was banned from appearing on the same stage as Paul Oakenfold for a good few years.

Sometimes, what we found funny internally wasn't received quite as warmly once it hit the shelves at WHSmith. Karl Hyde's "alcoholic" pull quote landed *Muzik* editor Ben Turner in hot water with Underworld's team—and the sweaty photo of Karl on the cover didn't help matters. But beyond the quotes themselves, the biggest source of contention was often the cover shot.

Artists frequently grumbled when they saw the final product in stores. Like *DJ Magazine* or *Jockey Slut*, *Muzik* never offered cover image approval to artists. Unless you were a superstar at the level of Tom Cruise or Madonna, no mainstream title in those days would allow an external team into their inner editorial sanctum. Artists would occasionally try to push past that barrier, but the policy remained firm—at least until relatively recently at *Mixmag* and *DJ Magazine*.

As I mentioned briefly, Ben Turner, along with Push, was the main editor of *Muzik* magazine in its early days, with Push staying for the first forty issues or so. The key thing to remember is just how influential the music press was at the time in making or breaking acts. We were the primary window to a world that hadn't yet reached mainstream culture. We had a job to do, and we wanted to do it well—but we also had a product to sell. Sometimes, all these factors collided on the same cover. And if we were too early in backing an artist, or if the artist wasn't as popular as, say, The Chemical Brothers, an issue could fall flat commercially, selling only half as many copies as the previous one—which no one wanted.

Ben Turner remembers this dynamic well, particularly when it came to *Muzik*'s cover featuring Underworld and the infamous pull quote about alcohol. "We were doing our jobs," Ben said of the decision. "The focus on the alcohol story tipped it over the edge and was a tough call to go to print on, but we had to do it. I learned then that, in this business, even your closest friends will take the bigger commercial opportunity when it comes to them. The interesting thing about the magazine market back then was that *Muzik* actually expanded the dance music sector—it helped *Mixmag* sell even more copies. If *Muzik* hit 50,000 sales, *Mixmag* was doing 80,000."

The DJ-baiting "Hang the DJ" back page, navigated by Ben and the team, struck a balance of humour and sharp commentary, closing each piece with the signature sign-off "Don't mess." It ran for over fifty issues before being quietly retired. If there's one thing we all learned during those years, it's that Detroit techno artists and rising UK producers didn't always share the same sense of humour we had at Hatfield House on Stamford Street.

When I flew to Ibiza, I was always put up at the El Divino Apartments, conveniently located next to a small, seemingly innocuous supermarket and a bar called Mezzanine. That bar was both the making and breaking of me that summer. If there was a party at Pacha, it was where we would end up afterward, as it was just a short stumble from the club.

Mezzanine became a haven for a British contingent of ravers I kept bumping into: Brandon Block and Alex P, Charlie Chester and his wife, producer Jo Mills (part of the early DC10/Circo-Loco clique alongside another UK DJ, Lottie), the big beat DJs Jon Carter and Derek Dahlarge, and my own raving crew, which included the mischievous identical twins Nigel and Ian Onwubalili, plus their ever-adventurous third wheel, Ricky Stoosh. There was also my curly-haired IPC/*Muzik* magazine photographer friend Debbie Bragg, who once spotted Frankie Knuckles in one of our favourite Italian restaurants in San Antonio and yelled, "FrankIEEE!" (I've never let her live that one down and never will, much to her annoyance).

One morning, I ended up at Mezzanine with Deep Dish and Boy George, who was very much in DJ mode that summer. [8] Away from the glare of the club, he seemed completely at home that morning and was in great spirits. For the record, I totally forgive him for pinching my bum and cackling the next time I saw him at Eden in San Antonio.

The main thing to remember about this era is just how cosmopolitan Ibiza was compared to Brighton, Birmingham, or

---

8 (D.D. fans may recall that Deep Dish would later go on to remix *Do You Really Want To Hurt Me*)

even Burgess Hill—and how potent proper house and techno could be when wielded by the right producer and DJ. That summer was emblematic of the American house invasion. Alongside Deep Dish, I also met Armand Van Helden at El Divino (we were wearing the same Nike sneakers—always a good icebreaker). While the French were beginning to infiltrate the scene, Americans like David Morales, Junior Sanchez, Roger Sanchez, and the Sound Factory heads Lord G and Harry 'Choo Choo' Romero led the production pack. They all treated Ibiza as the dance music mecca it was, with their careers often defined by the sets they played at 3 a.m.

Harry Romero's filter-disco house instrumental 'Tania' is the record I most associate with early CircoLoco, and Jo Mills—Charlie Chester's other half—seemed to hammer it relentlessly. Both Jo and Charlie remain staples on the island today, operating from their base in Santa Gertrudis. Jo also had her signature tune for the club: *Dancing in the Dark*.

Of course, despite the all-day house hedonism, Ibiza still had its rules. If you brought a camera to Space, they'd confiscate it for fear of anyone documenting the infamous terrace. My phone back then was a small blue Nokia, and while Ibiza was the most glamorous place on the planet—with Brits, Europeans, and American DJs mingling at clubs like Pacha, Privilege, and El Divino—only professional photographers carried quality cameras to capture the wildest moments. Andy McKay recently reminded me that clubs actively discouraged phones, as they preferred to sell "official" photos the next day—proof that commerce was always leading the way.

The quality of house music arriving from America at the time was unparalleled and one of the main reasons DJs were flown to Europe to play. Junior Sanchez's *B With U* was ubiquitous, and the excitement around records like that was palpable. Cool tracks would gain momentum in the clubs and, if they were big enough after dark, would eventually graze the outer edges of the UK Top 40.

Being at the epicentre of such a musically significant scene was thrilling. Ibiza was the place to be if you wanted to make it as a DJ or break a record in a club, bar, or after-party. Manumission often felt like the Cheers bar on a Monday night, where everyone from Norman Cook and Zoe Ball to Derek "Ceasefire" Dahlarge and a soon-to-be-suspended-from-the-BBC Lisa I'Anson could be found. If you were lucky, you might snag a "Guest Pass" for the Carry-On at Space. I vividly remember seeing Daft Punk DJing at a Manumission after-party there. They played Madonna's 'Holiday' mid-morning to much Balearic acclaim. While DC10 had started by then, it wasn't yet the hyped party it is now and mainly featured DJs like Cirillo and Clive Henry. Mondays were dominated by Manumission, with its pre-party in Ibiza Town, the main event hosted by Mike and Claire with 10,000 ravers, and the Tuesday morning Carry-On at Space before the festivities continued at Bora Bora until sundown.

Tuesdays were the workers' time to relax on the beach, where the best conversations often took place. Workers earned an average of 10,000 pesetas a week, though Claire Manumission recently told me she was earning 100,000 pesetas early on: "I was a damn good flyer girl!"

Ibiza will always be Ibiza. For some, it's now too commercial, derivative, and expensive, but for those of us who came of age there in the mid-'90s, it will forever hold a special place in our hearts. It was a jewel then, and while it remains one today, the price tag is considerably steeper than it was 25 years ago. So much of the island's magic was about feeling. While the main clubs were never cheap, venues like Space and Privilege offered something you simply couldn't find at your local pub in Portsmouth or Plymouth.

If you loved house music, as I did, you'd hear tracks months before they crossed into the mainstream. That sense of discovery was arguably my favourite part. Manumission's prestige in '99 and 2000 was at an all-time high, and I lost count of how many major players performed at Privilege for peanuts and drink tickets (often one and the same).

Things happened in Ibiza that I'm conveniently happy to forget—likely because it was 10 a.m. Mezzanine was often the go-to spot before or after a trip to the Space terrace, widely regarded as "the best club in the world." Ibiza's two pivotal clubs were Privilege and Space. Beyond Sundays, Space hosted brilliant polysexual parties like Café Olé on Mondays (which lasted 15 seasons) and Matinée on Saturday afternoons. More than anywhere else, Space was home to the beautiful people, only about 20% of whom were Brits. Everyone upped their game for Space: the girls, the dancers, and especially the DJs, who had to bring their best records or risk being outshone. Café Olé thrived on its reputation for extravagant productions, complete with dancers, acrobats, and artists of all kinds—it was Glitterbox before Glitterbox even existed.

Between Ibiza trips, I interviewed Creamfields acts for *Muzik* magazine at the Blackfriars office. Among them were American DJ Roger Sanchez and Blackpool's own Chris Lowe from the Pet

Shop Boys. Chris casually mentioned that he'd be visiting the island the following week, and I half-jokingly told him, "If I see you, I'll say hello." To my surprise, I did run into him at Bora Bora the next Monday afternoon, straight after Space. It was a serendipitous day filled with drinks, a trip to the old town to see Nancy Noise DJ, and finally a stint at Manumission, where I was pursuing a girl I liked. Chris and I both stayed until the end of the night, and 25 years later, we're still good friends. Over the years, I've commissioned remixes for the Pet Shop Boys from some of the best producers on the planet, including Carl Craig, Prins Thomas, Gerd Janson, and Marc "MK" Kinchen—the remix genius behind *Push the Feeling On* by The Nightcrawlers, one of the biggest club classics of all time.

As I write this in 2024, the truth remains the same as it was in '98 and '99: all roads lead back to Ibiza.

CHAPTER FIVE
PAPERBACK WRITER

It was August 1999 when Ben Turner rang my hotel one morning in Ibiza. I can still remember the call and message as clear as day:

"Hi Ralph, it's Ben Turner. You got the job."

I had been interviewed for a full-time staff position at *Muzik* along with around 18 other candidates earlier that summer. I honestly wasn't sure how well I'd come across in the interview. I still felt painfully new to the scene and, frankly, I looked up to Ben and Frank as London custodians of it. As far as I was concerned, I was slightly behind schedule on my career ladder—I was 24 and thought my life should have come together at least two years earlier! But what's always struck me since is how convinced I was that I'd find a job through the broadsheets' media section (translation: *The Guardian*'s Monday G2 pullout). The magical *Muzik* role I eventually landed hadn't even made it to print, let alone online.

It was an early reminder that life is about showing up, being present, and seeing what happens when you do. Although I had to overcome some existential shyness, this ethos has never left me: I still make it a point to go out at least three times a week to the right events!

I remember that *Muzik* interview as being incredibly important at the time—not just professionally, but also as one of life's biggest "Sliding Doors" moments. If I hadn't passed that particular hurdle and walked into Hatfield House, I probably wouldn't have become a Dance Music Lifer.

Getting my foot in the door at IPC not only paid me more than I'd ever earned before (I'd been on £120 a week at Round Sounds, most of which went to my horrified and terrified mum for rent), but it also came with a proper expense account. The same was true for Karen Young and our intrepid advertising friend Rebecca Walters, who would actually get told off by her Kings Reach bosses if she didn't spend enough on potential clients for the magazine's back pages.

I had my own desk, landline, and computer (those cute little Apple Macs from 1999 were the best) and instant access to a fax machine, which constantly burbled with incoming DJ charts all day. I was given business cards, made custodian of the Bedroom Bedlam DJ competition page, and soon after, the entire reviews section.

Although it wasn't long before Ben Turner announced his shock decision to leave the title for a new-fangled company called Worldpop (taking Rob da Bank with him and leaving Karen Young promoted to Clubs Editor), for my first few issues, *Muzik* ran like clockwork. The *Muzik* Awards were, at the time, essentially dance music's equivalent of the Oscars.

Sasha was honoured with the "Outstanding Contribution" award. The Breakthrough DJ in 1999 was Cheshire's finest, DJ Lottie—a rare win in an era dominated by white, middle-class male producers (plus ça change). The Chemical Brothers won

Best Live Act, Pete Tong hosted, and Norman and Zoe Ball lived up to their name, partying alongside the great and the good who flew in from around the world for one night only. Caners of the Year? After witnessing their antics in Ibiza, Alex P and Brandon Block were the perfect choice.

One of the most legendary pieces from this time was Andy Crysell's cover interview with Alexander Coe, aka Sasha. Andy, one of *Muzik*'s best writers and now a heavyweight in the advertising world, crafted an article that remains one of the most immortal pieces of electronic music journalism I've ever read. It left a lasting impression on me—not just as a journalist learning about style and storytelling but also as a reader realising I was part of something special, a unique culture in a unique time. The article ended with this gem of an exchange:

"I reckon he can talk to people through his music."
Sasha's driver, an irrepressibly chatty guy called Jem, is driving Muzik home, adding his thoughts to the table.
"When I return home to my mate's after a weekend with Sasha, I feel like I'm back on Earth after a weekend on Mars," Jem giggles.
The London sprawl slides into view, and he reveals he sometimes worries about his employer. "I hope he'll be OK. I hope he doesn't run out of money. Sometimes when I drop him off at his country house, I say, 'Are you sure you're alright out here?'"
"Yeah," he replies. "Just look at the stars."
"Haha, what a brilliant reply, eh?"

In short, while I don't think I could have arrived at a better time, try as I might, I never wrote a cover feature this good when I was under thirty.[1]

Now the founder of a cultural insights and innovation agency called Crowd DNA, young, erudite English writer Andy was arguably the most top-tier member of the magazine's entire editorial team. Even all these years later, this outro paragraph still makes me wistful. (He ran so we could walk!)

What I especially loved about this era of the print magazine was that it was a fully formed, well-oiled machine that knew how to work at speed (*at* speed, not *on* speed). Covers and ideas seemed to come together with such effortlessness that it was only when you peered behind the curtain that you realised how much hard work went into ensuring the feature flow was varied and well-written, and that the magazine's much-vaunted reviews section came together in time for deadline.

There were also far more women writing for the title than you'd typically see in dance media: Bethan Cole and Emma Warren were both regular contributors. And while we weren't exclusively obsessed with house and techno—though, let's be honest, they were our primary focus since UK clubs were hammering those records the most—*Muzik* still made space for jungle, trip-hop, soul, R&B, and (whisper it) trance. Yes, a very orange Paul Van Dyk once got the cover, much to Karen's chagrin, as I recall. That said, we'd also featured Judge Jules[2] on the cover earlier that

---

[1] Maybe I got pretty close at *Mixmag* when I got to the heart of what makes Kölsch tick in Copenhagen but that's more up to him than for me to say.

[2] (ironically, now my lawyer)

year, clearly because Ben was bullish about *Muzik* competing with *Mixmag*, whose mindset in this era was more commercially driven. Make no mistake, though: *Mixmag* was the market leader, and despite our early PLUR idealism, business was business.

September 1999 also saw London welcome two new clubs, almost simultaneously. Well, perhaps *welcome* isn't the right word, as these clubs were often viewed by the authorities as dens of iniquity and hedonism rather than house music meccas. Thanks to Ben Turner, and whether it was the right move or not, *Muzik* put Paul Oakenfold on the cover to celebrate the opening of home in Leicester Square. In retrospect, while it might not have been the perfect decision, rivals fabric were on the backfoot in terms of timing. Fabric had experienced some teething problems and didn't open until October.

As a 25-year-old Londoner at the end of 1999, I suddenly had some of the best clubs on the planet on my doorstep. Not only fabric and Home, but also Turnmills in Farringdon and The End on West Central Street—not to mention The Cross, The Key, and Canvas.

Please don't ask me to pick between the first four because they all brought something different to the table, though The End and fabric shared a very similar underground ethos. The End was all about Laurent Garnier, Layo & Bushwacka!, Mr. C, Derrick Carter, Deep Dish, and Carl Cox. Fabric, by contrast, was broadly less concerned with the global icons Ben and I loved (Garnier, Hawtin, Danny Tenaglia, Carl Cox, and LTJ Bukem) and more focused on UK-centric techno talent, such as their London-based residents Terry Francis and Craig Richards, who, to their credit, have gone the distance and still play the main room of the club today.

Turnmills was the home of Tall Paul, as well as Brighton club bastions like Big Beat Boutique and a rolling revue of Skint and Wall of Sound talent, including Theo Keating of The Wiseguys, Jon Carter, and The Chemical Brothers. It wasn't long, however, before licensing problems led to home in Leicester Square closing for good. Most weekends after that, I would club-hop between The End and fabric, which is probably why I now possess a shiny fabric membership card in 2024. In moments of whimsy, I like to think of it as representing 25 years of invisible rave service.

As home gave birth to the next stage in Paul Oakenfold's career (let's call this the *Bullet in the Gun* era—yikes), and future Madonna producer Jacques Lu Cont and Tim Sheridan began making waves, over at fabric, a new fiercely underground ethos was emerging. At the opening of Home, a shiny new nightclub in Leicester Square launched by the forthright former Cream boss Darren Hughes, Rod Stewart and Ronnie Wood strolled in ahead of me; at fabric, they wouldn't have made it past the bouncers. The line-up that opening weekend was a who's who of the London underground scene, including Sasha, Adam Freeland, and Dave Mothersole. Breakbeat was breaking through to the mainstream, and it wasn't long before The Plump DJs were remixing The Doors.

I was being paid to attend top-tier events, not just in London but, in the years that followed, in Sydney, Miami, Las Vegas, Brazil, Germany, France, and beyond—an endless list of countries discovering acid house. One of the best trips in those early days was to Buenos Aires, Argentina, where my friend Martín Gontad managed Hernán Cattáneo and ran Pacha in the region. I'd return later with Fatboy Slim, and I still have the blurry club photos to prove it. South America had been early adopters of Sasha, Digweed, and the progressive house sound—now enjoying another resurgence with a new generation. In that era, however, a four-page feature in a magazine carried more weight than almost anything else. (Only radio had a similar impact, which is why Pete Tong's *Essential Mix* was such an important barometer of musical and touring success. Look at the *Essential Mix* from 1995 to 2005, and you'll see that every notable DJ of the time added it as a career milestone.)

Of all the clubs I frequented during my *Muzik* years, fabric is the only one still standing. In 2019, the club turned 20, and they celebrated two decades with the following statement: *"We've stuck to our mission over the years, and the disco has taken on a life of its own. Three nights per week, every week, for the last two decades. Never not making noise."*

Of all the clubs still operating in the city—and let's not forget the original Ministry of Sound on Gaunt Street, still thriving after all these years—fabric is the one that still truly has my heart. A recently written book by Joe Muggs brilliantly details the club's ups and downs, but the fact that it's still here is all that really matters. My friend Ailsa and I recently spent a very memorable Sunday afternoon in Room 2 dancing to Dixon and Ben Klock, and it really was quite magical. London needs fabric. And in this city, fabric and I share the same 'rave age'—25!

CHAPTER SIX
MUZIK IS THE ANSWER

"We wanted to give an identity to dance music that wasn't fluffy bras or cheesy DJs."

Christopher Dawes / Push, April 2024

"Muzik was how people learned the stories behind the most influential electronic music artists in the world. What Chef's Table has done for humanising the personalities of decorated chefs, we did the same for DJs thirty years ago."

Ben Turner, May 2024

I'm going to say it loud now because if I don't, I doubt anyone else will: those first 50 or so issues of *Muzik* magazine—aside from maybe the Ballistic Brothers cover misstep (which Ben Turner definitely still has creative misgivings about)—were brilliantly curated publications that, for the most part, editorially stand up even today. While *Muzik* magazine started in 1995, this chapter is, in many ways, the heart of this book. I wouldn't be writing this music memoir at all if it weren't for my time in the trenches there in the late '90s: it ignited in me a passion not just for quality underground music but also for an across-the-board appreciation of jungle, soul, techno, and, if I was in a generous mood, even the odd moment of trance.

Every single month, that magazine was a breath of fresh air, and if I didn't devote a whole chapter to the story of its birth, I'd never forgive myself. I also wouldn't be doing the job I do now in the industry if it weren't for my tenure there. And given that no one else has written in detail about *Muzik* magazine in the last 20 years, I've taken it upon myself to do it justice in print.

"I did a week's work experience at *Melody Maker* when I was 16," says Ben Turner when we catch up midway through 2024, reflecting on his impossibly early start in publishing. "I got sucked into electronic music very quickly and soon discovered that only Push and a handful of (important) others had any idea what I was talking about. I started compiling a column called *Twilight Zone* for the *Maker*. It was a club listings column, but I'd rant and rave about DJs and records that had exploded at institutions like Club 69 in Paisley or Sabresonic in London.

"To this small handful of us at the time, these DJs were as exciting as watching any rock band perform. I was never a great writer—I didn't have the university schooling like so many at *Melody Maker* and *NME* seemed to have—but I wrote with passion and conviction. I had the instinct and belief that DJ culture would change the world. I felt that way about Carl Cox, Richie Hawtin, Danny Tenaglia, and Laurent Garnier. I watched them meticulously, over and over again.

"I felt and saw something that changed the way people experienced music, initially from the dancefloor and, quite quickly, from the DJ booth. To this day, I still regularly get people all over the world thanking me for the impact of the magazine on their lives."

In essence, *Muzik* gave mid-'90s electronic music a proper vocal and visual identity, but it was the team that ensured every element adhered to strict journalistic standards. While *Mixmag* in the same era might snag an album scoop with an artist like The Prodigy or Moby, *Muzik* may not have been the biggest, but it was undoubtedly the best. That was down to incredible editorial teamwork, which started as a kernel of an idea between Push, Ben Turner, and a couple of key players from IPC's suit department.

We'll get to that in a hot minute, but ultimately what we're talking about here is killer curation with a huge dollop of passion. Because ultimately, what drove *Muzik* was pure passion.

"It's at the top of the pile," says Push proudly (who prefers this pseudonym for his writing and still uses it today) when we discuss what *Muzik* magazine means to him in terms of his overall career as a music writer, curator, and editor. "What we pulled off was very, very special, and I must stress that everybody was important."

But how did it begin?

"It was a weird one," says Push slowly. "So the quick answer is, we didn't go to them... they came to us."

For the next part of the story, we need to go back to 1994, when Ben Turner and Push were working for *Melody Maker* at IPC Media, situated on the 26th floor of Kings Reach Tower on Stamford Street. The *NME* team was one floor below. Stamford Street, conveniently close to Waterloo and Blackfriars stations, offered a bevy of boozers nearby that helped stoke and fuel that early inspiration. [1] But I'll let Push take over my book for a moment, since I was still in my first year at Warwick University when that genuinely iconic *Underworld* cover landed on an unsuspecting campus one Wednesday in 1994.

"Ben was quite new," remembers Push, who not only interviewed Laurent Garnier at *Muzik* but also a nascent Nirvana for the weekly before making that all-important giant leap to the dance scene. "He started helping out in the picture library and also did work experience—and didn't actually leave! Ben got on well with Steve Sutherland, who was deputy editor of *Melody Maker* then. Everyone liked Ben. So Ben and I worked together for *Melody Maker* in '94. I'd been at *Melody Maker* since 1985, whereas he was still really, really young. I was writing a lot about hip hop and rock, but when acid house happened, I was right in the middle of that, and it was a huge thing for me. After a year or two, I convinced *Melody Maker* to let us have a dance music section, which was always a page or two. We did that with Andy Smith, another journalist there, and Bob Stanley from Saint Etienne. Then Bob left the paper as Saint Etienne was happening, so it was down to me, Andy Smith, and [tech-house DJ] Dave Mothersole, who joined a little later, and we did that for a year and a half."

However, a reader survey nearly scuppered these best-laid plans. "Yes. *Melody Maker* did a reader survey and, as a result, they actually dropped the dance music page! One of the questions in this survey was: *Do you want more coverage of dance music?*

---

[1] The biggest and best was called Doggetts and it's still there on the very edge of Blackfriars Bridge.

But what IPC did was this: everyone who wrote in was given a chance to win a load of freebies, and a lot of it was Guns N' Roses stuff. So only rock fans entered, and no dance fans contributed to the survey! Dance music was always hard to get into *Melody Maker*—the editor, Allan Jones, was sympathetic, but the majority of writers were into indie. It was exactly the same at *NME*. Then, as we got into the '90s—and there were always turning points along the way—the real turning point was the first Underworld album. That came out in January 1994, and *Melody Maker* did a dance music special with Underworld on the cover. I wrote the Underworld piece, and we did something like 16 pages on dance music, which, for *Melody Maker*, was a big chunk."

Ben Turner wrote the lead album review in this issue—a huge commission at the time for him. The album, *dubnobasswithmyheadman*, went Top 10 in the UK album charts that week. "We felt we'd made a huge difference—for a rock paper to visibly chart an electronic act, albeit one that seamlessly used guitars. We went to the Stamford Arms pub to celebrate at lunch, but my joy was interrupted by my mentor Steve Sutherland (by now *NME*'s editor), who told me that our elevated coverage of dance music would bury the *Maker* into the ground, that sales would be a disaster."

In that same iconic Underworld issue, the paper also featured interviews with Orbital, The Orb, The Drum Club, and a young, emerging Aphex Twin. The *Maker* quickly gained a reputation in the techno community for having its finger on the pulse, which, in turn, saw the legendary independent Belgian dance label R&S Records book a run of double-page adverts. "No one apart from the dance heads at the *Maker* had heard of R&S," remembers Ben with a smile. "It was at that point that IPC thought, *Hang on a minute, why are these dance labels spending money in a rock paper?*"

Ben warms to the theme. "There was something very special going on in the UK around clubs and DJ culture, and my *Twilight Zone* column became integrated into a new dance section which Push and I edited called *Orbit*. Allan Jones walked over to me and said, *I don't understand a word of what Orbit is about, but keep on doing it!* No major label had advertised in these hallowed centre pages for some time. Our weekly three-to-four-page section became a vital source of discovery for dedicated fans of dance music around the world. I was 19 years old at this point. I was a music fan who came in via work experience at *Melody Maker* and very quickly fell in love with dance music, watching DJs every night of the week and coming back to the office with a new language, enthusing about DJs 'dropping' records! However, there was constant pushback from some quarters, which fueled my passion for this music for life. I still get it today. The challenges are different now that it's become a $13 billion industry. But people still have a negative perception of the culture."

"They were quite clever," adds Push, referring to the choice of the distinctive Underworld cover image, which featured Karl Hyde, Rick Smith, and future *Muzik* DJ and production star Darren Emerson. The cover's main sell described it as "the big bang: Underworld and the new dance explosion." Alongside Weatherall and One Dove, the feature also included pieces on The Grid, Moby, Orbital, D:Ream, Inner City, and Youth. Back to Push: "That specific picture of Underworld—Karl was holding a guitar—made it OK for people who didn't know Underworld [and were probably rock fans]. But they were still fairly unknown and specialist to a *Melody Maker* audience. It was a great cover, a big, long piece, and they were great to interview, as you know!"

After that issue's success, the following week they launched *Orbit*. The innovative and future-facing club section quickly gained a reputation for having its finger on the proverbial pulse. Artists who featured in *Orbit* included future legends like Larry Heard and Planet E DJ/producer Carl Craig. Back to Push: "One day, the publisher, Alan Lewis, came to both of us and said, *We are thinking about a dance music magazine. Can we have a meeting?* That was February or March 1994, and it was Alan who came up with the idea. We started working on it straight away. We did two dummy issues and started talking to people on the quiet. We had a room with photos we'd nicked from *Melody Maker*, and there were a couple of focus groups getting people in. We had James Lavelle on the cover of the first dummy issue (although that got no further than photocopied pages in a folder), while the second was a printed dummy issue with Jon Pleased Wimmin on the cover. We had 1,000 copies of that one."

"Alan Lewis was the Editor-in-Chief of all the music titles, and he was a fantastic bloke. He'd launched the (boldly titled) *Black Music Magazine* in the '70s and had been the editor of *Sounds* and *NME*. He also launched *Kerrang!*, *Vox*, *Loaded*, and then *Muzik*. At the time, IPC Media was doing loads of new launches, and Andy McDuff was the publishing director." These are important names in this story: despite ostensibly being what we juniors would call suits, without them, the magazine would never have gotten off the ground. Andy joined IPC in 1977 and left in 2000. He later became managing director of Metropolis

International for many years before retiring from the magazine industry. Sadly, Alan Lewis, a very hands-on but brilliant editor, passed away in 2021, aged 75, from Parkinson's disease and cancer. His 45-year career in publishing and flair for smart recruitment should never be forgotten.

Back to Push: "So they came to Ben and me, and we put together 'dummies' as everyone liked the concept. Then they brought on Bruce Sandell (who later became associate publisher of *Muzik* and *Uncut*) to do the advertising. Between us and Brett Lewis, the art editor, we put it all together. It was terrifying!"

Did they think it would be a success?

"We had no idea. We were confident up to a point, but we had no idea. You're in the lap of the gods!"

Says Ben: "We were placed in a secret office and weren't allowed to explain to anybody what we were working on, all while not knowing if our time would result in our own title. By launching *Muzik* as a monthly to rival *Mixmag*, we would lose the frequency of the weekly rock press, which allowed us to be so responsive to new music. I'd hear a new Detroit record in a club or at Fat Cat on the weekend and review it for the issue out four days later! Losing that immediacy was scary—I was obsessed with our column being cutting-edge."

That first issue of *Muzik*, with Tom and Ed Chemical on the cover, was for sale at Tribal Gathering in 1995 and on newsstands across the country. In the mid-1990s, such publications wielded incredible power to discuss and break artists. The Chemical Brothers set the tone perfectly—a credible British duo on the rise.

"My memory is that we had The Chemical Brothers issue in the bag," recalls Push. "I remember that because I did the interview.

CHAPTER SIX: MUZIK IS THE ANSWER

We knew Tribal Gathering was happening, so we had a stall there. I think we were selling the magazine rather than giving it away, but at the end, whatever was left, we gave away. They were handing them out to people on the way out because they didn't want to take the boxes home. My other memory is that it was cheap—95p!"

But what readers might not know is that Tom and Ed really weren't happy with the piece.

"The Chemical Brothers got upset about the cover feature I wrote," recalls Push with a slight wince. "They were very critical of the dance music scene during the interview—and they were bloody right in what they said—but I don't think they expected me to put it all in the feature. They didn't tell me not to use any of it! We launched the magazine properly at Tribal Gathering, and that's where Tom and Ed saw the article for the first time. They were so furious about what I'd written that they threw the mag on the floor and stamped all over it. They hated what I'd written. They said things they seemed to regret later and were pissed off with me and *Muzik*. When I went backstage, Ben came up to me and said, 'Keep away from The Chems.' That was 1995. I've never written a single word about The Chemical Brothers since then. I still love them, but I suspect they still hate me."

And the name?

As acid house and techno bubbled up, the usually sleepy suits at IPC really started paying attention. With *Orbit* established as *Melody Maker*'s dance music section, they needed a title for the new dance music magazine. "We had endless meetings trying to come up with a name," remembers Push. "We settled on *Muzik* because it seemed a bit futuristic and opened the opportunity for us not to be just a dance music magazine. *Muzik* was a 'blank canvas' name—it was meant to deal with whatever the latest exciting thing was. But once we launched, we realised we had a problem because, when you said the title—especially on the phone or the radio—you always had to say, *Muzik—with a Z and a K*. It was 1995, but we wanted a 21st-century name. I have no idea who came up with it. I remember saying in meetings with Andy and Alan that if we did *Muzik* right, there's no reason it couldn't be the *NME* of the 21st century. It didn't need to be a dance music magazine forever. I thought there was a music revolution every ten years, and I was excited by what would happen at the end of the 1990s. Drum 'n' bass wasn't the revolution that acid house had been—it's been more subtle than explosive. And that was good."

Ben shares a similar view. "It was all in the name. It was ALL about the music—certainly initially. It represented where Push and I came from. We wanted to critique dance music the same way the rock press critiqued rock. This approach was something many in the dance music industry couldn't initially understand."

The covers were immaculate, the features scintillating, and the full-page reviews definitive. If your favourite genre mattered, you got a full page devoted to the latest releases. If you were an artist on the rise, you'd be discussed and dissected, eventually landing a print cover and an eight-page spread. Most of all, *Muzik* offered a new, critical, and engaged take on music itself.

"I think that's what we were trying to do," agrees Push. "Every magazine is chaotic. But you're doing the best you can. Your enthusiasm runs away with you, and you don't sleep for two days. But everyone pulls in the same direction because you want to represent it in the best way possible. That's where we came from.

CHAPTER SIX: MUZIK IS THE ANSWER

We applied the same learning from *Melody Maker* and *NME*, and those were bear pits! You had to fight to be heard. We learned toughness from that and reviewed DJs in the same way as bands. Girls in fluffy bras were part of the scene, but we wanted an in-depth appraisal of the music and DJs as artists creating soundscapes on the night. What tools did they use to make those nights work? And sometimes, it didn't work—and you had to say that. It was the rock music approach to dance music."

Ben makes an excellent point as we wrap up our first conversation. "We pushed *Mixmag* to become a better magazine," he says. "We had *Mixmag* and *DJ Magazine* as competitors, but *Mixmag* just didn't speak to me about the music I was discovering. I remember *Mixmag* doing a four-page feature on DJs going fishing and being so angry! I valued music and critical music journalism. Simon Reynolds, The Stud Brothers, David Stubbs, Andy Smith, Steve Sutherland—these were the last generation of powerful, poetic, poignant writers.

Muzik quickly became the place to learn about the stories behind the most influential electronic music artists in the world. What *Chef's Table* and Netflix have done for humanising chefs, *Muzik* did for DJs thirty years ago. For some reason, artists really opened up to me, which I value most looking back. Carl Cox entrusted me with his revelatory cover story about hidden racism in early London club culture—a personal, powerful, and provocative story. He chose to do that with *Muzik*, as did so many others."

In July 1995, *Muzik*'s second issue dropped on campus. I remember seeing that cover vividly on the shelves. This time, the cover star was American superstar DJ Junior Vasquez, who was admired by Brits like the Boys Own collective—possibly because he hammered so many of their tunes at the iconic Sound Factory in New York. Vasquez was starting to make a name for himself with artists like Madonna, referenced on his infamous single *If Madonna Calls*.

But there were further teething problems.

"Again, the roundabout goes round and round and never stops," says Push, recalling issue two. "We were near the end of the second issue—and we changed the design at the last minute and had at least two all-nighters getting the Vasquez feature re-designed—but three weeks in, Ben stopped me in the corridor and said we have the initial sales figures for the first issue. I thought he said 13,000. And I said, 'That's not good.' He said, 'No, no, 30,000!' I don't know what we were aiming for, but 30,000—we hit that, and by the time we were off sale, we had hit 40,000. Issue 2 went down a bit, but we picked up with Dave Clarke on issue three and Carl Cox on issue four—strong covers with strong people, particularly Coxy.

"So we settled on 35-40,000 for the first year or so. Issues three and four were more experimental, but we'd got the momentum going. Issue five was Roger Sanchez, which dipped a bit, but by the time we got to Christmas and the December issue, we did Goldie, Leftfield, and Paul Oakenfold, and by that point, we felt we were established and that IPC were keen to carry on. Six months in, Push and Ben were offered full-time contracts on the title: 'And that's when we first knew it was going to work.'"

I was still at university, eagerly waiting for each issue to arrive on campus, and when it did, that meant an exciting afternoon lost in 100+ pages of electronic absorption. Early cover stars included Josh Wink, Inner City, and Brian 'BT' Transeau, an issue I distinctly remember reading on the day it came out when I really should have been paying attention in class. But in many ways, I was being schooled in a different way: I was being educated by the best electronic magazine on the shelf and the brilliantly snarky catchphrase on the back page of 'Hang The DJ': "Don't mess!"

Calvin Bush was also instrumental in getting both myself and Rob da Bank through the door. And like me, Robby is a little bit evangelical about his years behind the *Muzik* desk, first on work experience and eventually as Assistant Editor. "I loved seeing how a magazine was put together," he says. "Pre-social media, you got your news from a magazine, and I worked my way up from picture editor to Assistant Editor and did most jobs on the mag. What I loved were people like Calvin Bush—who was a bit like a headmaster and would give me a dressing down about my grammar—but that's because it wasn't a throwaway mag, it was put together in an amazing way. As Picture Editor, I knew Ben had high standards, and so did Calvin. My low point was writing a review of Lauryn Hill's solo album *The Miseducation of Lauryn Hill*; I gave it a pasting because Calvin said, 'You're too nice about everything!' I gave it 2 out of 5, and Ben said, 'Are you sure?' and I said, 'Yes!' I learned my lesson the hard way, and most importantly, Calvin taught me how to write. I was the reviews editor for a while, and I loved that. You're dealing with people like Terry Farley and Dave Mothersole—total experts in their field—every day, chatting with encyclopaedic minds of dance music in every genre."

"Calvin Bush was a wild one," remembers Ben of the magazine's unpredictable but always entertaining, unflappable Reviews

Editor, who left in late 1999 to start a career as a lawyer. "He was writing for us at Orbit for Melody Maker, and one night we were at Sabresonic, really drunk, and he whispered in my ear, 'You do know I write for NME under another name.' I couldn't believe his front! I don't think anyone else ever pulled that off in the competitive rock press wars! There were always moments like that with Calvin around, but he was a brilliant writer. Calvin was our wordsmith."

"Calvin Bush was an incredible writer," agrees Push. "In fact, I keep asking him to write for me now at Electronic Sound, but he won't do it! He's still a lawyer.

"Calvin was at Melody Maker before, and we also had David Stubbs, Mark Roland, and Martin James from MM too. Beyond those names, we attracted other people in. Sonia Poulton was brilliant on hip-hop, Rupert Howe was writing about drum 'n' bass, Jacqueline Springer was writing about urban stuff, and Jonty Adderley was doing reportage features. Bethan Cole came over to us from Mixmag, and we had Rachel Newsome and Emma Warren come in too. We attracted them."

Now a serial entrepreneur with Bestival, a constantly chugging DJ career, and a still-successful esoteric indie label called Sunday Best under his belt, young Rob da Bank also brought a new brand of off-the-wall irreverence and humour to the magazine, and it's no surprise that he looks back on his formative years with real fondness. "You dislike your main competitor," says Robby, referring to *Mixmag* and, to a certain degree, *DJ Magazine*. "*Muzik* was always classy, even in the humour... the journalism was a step above most other magazines, and Ben and Push really did bring together the best team out there. And I have to say, Andy Crysell was a phenomenal writer. Standing around Brett and Paul Allen, I loved that bit, deciding on a cover, arguing over a strapline. So much effort went into everything. DJ and Mixmag would be cheaper somehow. I still read Mixmag, DJ, and Jockey Slut—they're brilliant magazines—but we felt we were in a different class."

It's only 25 years later that I can see the influence the magazine had on my young mind. Certain artists would appear on the pages again and again—not just The Chemical Brothers, but Paul Oakenfold, Sasha and Digweed, DJ Rap, Fatboy Slim, Fabio and Grooverider (he got a solo cover when he signed to Columbia), and even Tall Paul, and every single one of them is still blazing a trail today, albeit in a place somewhere in between the madness of youth and the safety of heritage. Ben Turner would be instrumental in bringing the likes of Underworld and Faithless to wider attention, and from the sidelines, I would also be asked to review the latter's second album 'Sunday 8PM' and Norman's multi-million-selling '…Baby' via a promo cassette in 1998. And then there was Deep Dish, who were also styled by Vincent McDonald and gave zero fucks in their interview copy, which nearly resulted in a lawsuit. Just listen to *Muzik* magazine's 'Compilation of the Year' (1995), the incomparable 'Penetrate Deeper,' and you'll soon hear why it's the definition of timeless. But by this point—November 1996—Ali and Sharam were flying. Now signed to Deconstruction, their first LP *Junk Science* would also spawn the iconic single *Future Of The Future* with Everything But The Girl's Tracey Thorn on vocals. By this point, Ben's feature writing was totally on point, and I can still remember laughing at their occasional rants.

In many ways, one of the most quintessential nineties dance acts of the mid-nineties was the BMG-signed dance quartet Faithless. It was Pete Tong who insisted that the band release *Insomnia* from their debut album, and that track eventually peaked at number 3 in the UK charts, an incredible result for an era full of Robson & Jerome, Babylon Zoo, and Take That. Ben Turner cultivated a close relationship with the band, and Sister Bliss remembers that first Faithless cover from '96. "What a great magazine *Muzik* was," she remembers. "It gave us huge support and exposure. I can even remember what I was wearing for our first shoot—it was a Paul Smith suit!"

The ads pages were also growing. I found an early report for *Muzik* online as part of my research for this book, and it sums up the confidence of the era nicely. It's from *The Media Leader*, November 1995: "IPC is claiming that *Muzik*, its specialist dance title, has taken the majority share in the record company advertising within the dance music magazine market after just five issues. *Muzik* holds 41% of all advertising from this market, as well as a significant amount from the club sector. IPC claims it has brought in a considerable amount of new revenue for the IPC Music Group as a whole."

Muzik's advertising manager, Bruce Sandell, said that *Muzik* had revenue at 154% and paging at 105% above plan. "We have generated 128 pages of new business for the total IPC Music Group." The title is also building revenue from consumer advertising sectors with bookings from K-Cider, Sony Playstation, COI Blood, Caterpillar Boots, and Canadian Club."

There are plenty of other aspects to the magazine that we'll get to later. One section I was involved in, Bedroom Bedlam, helped launch DJs like Radio Slave, Yousef, and James Zabiela. "We did so much more than just put a magazine out," says Ben. There was also Ben's *Ibiza: Inspired Images From The Island Of Dance* book for Random House, and after every summer, the annual *Muzik* Awards and the supporting tour with SJM Concerts. These took place every October and were made in association with BBC Radio 1. Pete Tong was integral as the host (later joined by Zoe Ball), Frankie Knuckles flew in from New York for the second awards ceremony in Bristol, and in later years, you'd see everyone from Goldie, Kate Moss, and Noel Gallagher to Daft Punk and Carl Cox milling around.

When I look at the first few issues, from The Chemical Brothers to Laurent Garnier (both shot and executed by Vincent McDonald, as was the classic Danny Tenaglia waterski shoot in the sea opposite Mambo & Cafe del Mar), I'm transported back to a time and place where Turnmills and The End ruled the roost in London, Junior Vasquez dominated New York, and Dave Clarke was coming into his own via *Red 2* as The Baron of Techno. What Muzik did better than any other publication was represent the scene and the artists in a way that was equal parts serious and playful, and the covers – including one of Daft Punk turned into frogs on lily pads – were at their best, iconic and timeless. (The Daft Punk as frogs on lily pads (GEDDIT!) is probably the one most people remember from this era, but I remember that Christmas cover featuring Paul Oakenfold, Goldie, and Leftfield, which I saw one festive season at Bristol train station and bought immediately.) The covers pulled you into a wider world of techno trainspotting, just as they were designed to, and Vincent's iconic images are a huge part of why the artists covet their magazine covers almost three decades later.

"We wanted to make these people look good and look cool," says Push of those era-defining editorial decisions. "Vincent had been a freelancer for *NME* but came out of the same world. We had to find our own people. I lived in Brentford and would get the train into Waterloo. When I was at *Melody Maker*, I would do that three times a week and buy the *Guardian* for *Past Notes*. It was a tiny column in the back of the second section. I had realized while travelling that if you make a tiny thing really good, people will buy it for that, whether it's for *Hang The DJ* or whatever it is. And then you've got them!"

"The early issues were pre-email and internet, so we did everything via fax," adds Ben. "And this was how people learned the stories of some of the most influential artists in the world. Our whole mantra was – tell us your story."

Crucially, there wasn't any filler.

The *Trainspotting* pages, written by the likes of Dreem Teem star Spoony, Bob Jones, Terry Farley, Kevin McKay, and Will Ashon (who would later start Big Dada Records and sign Roots Manuva, among many others), were peerless in their taste and field: they were all club connoisseurs keen to display their stripes.

"We always set out to have the *Trainspotting* pages," continues Push. "It's not just going to be house and techno. It was important to have hip-hop reviews, and we had Will Ashon doing those. I didn't know who he was initially; maybe he'd been at a fanzine, but we loved his enthusiasm, and we did that a lot – hiring people with real passion. We made a point of making it as broad as possible, and that included soul music. Our thinking was – when you go to a club and you have a good time, when you come home, you don't listen to that music all the time, you might put on some old stuff or even some rock stuff. Someone like Seefeel. And we did that with *Electronic Sound* – people using guitars in a different way: making people ask, is that a guitar or a synth?"

Push is now running the still-in-print and thriving monthly *Electronic Sound* magazine for an older, plugged-in electronic audience, but what shines through in our conversation is how kind and considerate he remains and what an impact he accidentally had on many people's lives.

Beyond myself and Rob da Bank, I'd argue that Push and Ben Turner helped pave the way for credible coverage in dance music in a way that *Mixmag* and *DJ* just couldn't quite manage in the 1990s. Without them and *Muzik*, it's unlikely that writers like Emma Warren or Dorian Lynskey would have travelled as far as they have without their early electronic commissions to spur them on.

"We really did shine a light on music that wasn't being championed anywhere else," says Ben Turner. "The electronic world suffers from a serious lack of a single authoritative voice today. For about six years, we certainly felt *Muzik* was that voice."

But in 1995, *Muzik* stood out and stood firm. And the covers were a huge part of the DNA, overall identity, and ultimately sales tactics. These days, making a decent stab at Photoshop is par for the course, but back then, when cameras still used film, what Vincent and others did each month on the front pages inside of *Muzik* was incredible. "The front covers were hugely important," believes Ben. "We were treating underground artists like Dave Clarke or Fabio like rock stars. I'd also credit Raise-A-Head

(Adrian Batty) and Jamie B (Baker) with shooting DJs and clubs through a unique lens at that time. We had a very reactive audience, and it was great to see that we could help artists sell records. I was obsessed with making sure we were so on the money with our A&R. *Muzik* really was many people's education."

Muzik was my postgraduate education too.

In 2024, Ben is far more bullish than anyone else from the editorial team about the impact of the magazine. "So much went on at *Melody Maker* and *Muzik* that helped build the foundations of the genre that is clearly mainstream culture today," he says. "The battles we had with the traditional music and media industry about taking DJs and electronic music seriously were at times vicious, personal, and sometimes violent! The hardest thing for me to come to terms with at the time was building such a strong relationship with the artist community but then poking at them for making bad records in the magazine. Generally, the rock press said whatever the f*** they wanted with no consequence. I got close to so many of the artists. At one point, Carl Cox and his wife were renting a spare room in my Tower Bridge apartment as a bolthole for his London club residency. It was at times innocently incestuous, but only because we were all on the same mission to succeed and grow the art form." The most sensitive being, of course, the back-page *Hang The DJ* feature, where we would lambast an artist we felt had simply gone too far: no one was off-limits.

Muzik was a success story, and everyone wanted in, but the team didn't so much outgrow their first office on the 25th floor of IPC's King's Reach Tower alongside *NME* and *Vox* Magazine, as get kicked out due to the constant thud of techno. Their new home was over the road, in Hatfield House, in an office next door to *Loaded* magazine, which IPC had launched a few months before *Muzik* – and this was where I would find that incredible, fully-formed team in 1998, aged just 24, and still impossibly shy in that regional English way that so many eighties kids were. I had a lot to learn.

"Most of our behavioural fun and madness was in clubs around the world," says Ben, looking back. "We were actually quite studious in the office. We got our heads down to get the magazine out, while at *Loaded* it was utter chaos. There was always a party going on next door. I think they all thought we were really boring! Little did they know…"

In 1999, Rob da Bank and I were both sent to Ibiza to work on a joint *Muzik* and *Loaded* title called *The Islander*. Still the likeable, musical character he was when I first met him back in 1998, Robby was only too happy to chat about his career-kick starting time at the magazine. Twenty-five years on, he says that he didn't actually want to be a music journalist. "I'm a jack of all trades!" he says today. "The only thing I said was I wanted to be a journalist, and I fell into *Muzik* magazine. My first job was working for Mark Jones at Wall of Sound, and that was when Big Beat was exploding. As well as Skint and the Big Beat Boutique, I was also going to raves at Heaven with Fabio and Grooverider and running Sunday Best, my party and record label. I unashamedly loved Big Beat and went to *Muzik* for a two-week work placement and stayed for 7 or 8 years. I never intended on staying, but once I started, I got an appetite for it."

Other notable figures who started at *Muzik* magazine include future *Dazed & Confused* editor Rachel Newsome ("she was so young and smart and worked hard to help us evolve," says Ben), double Mercury Award-winning Big Dada label boss Will Ashon, no-nonsense tabloid journalist Sonia Poulton, Kris Needs, (Dr.) Bob Jones (one of British dance music's longest-serving selectors and a key part of the UK's soul and jazz dance then and now), monthly garage reviewer Spoony, and breakbeat and hardcore hero Slipmatt. The magazine's tech editor was *Electronic Sound*'s now-deputy editor Mark Roland, which just goes to show how much importance was placed on quality. Refreshingly, *Muzik* was not a boy's club, and the breadth of music covered was close to *Jockey Slut*, but while they were Manchester through and through, *Muzik* looked to the world. Ben Turner would head to Argentina to discover the exploding South American scene, and Bob Jones would be called upon to review Erykah Badu's debut album. Muzik also put Badu on the cover long before she exploded as a neo-soul icon, and alongside Erykah, Muzik kept an eye on the ever-growing French invasion of Daft Punk, Air, La Funk Mob, and Cassius.

Ben remembers a few other key players. "Yousef, Karen Young, and Robby, these were all beautiful careers to watch happen. I think about the contributions of freelancers Sonia Poulton and Will Ashon— with their help, we created a world where the Wu-Tang Clan exclusives could sit next to Juan Atkins and The Chemical Brothers. It was so great that the magazine could cover hip hop and UK garage as well as house and techno. Push and I never relied on external PR companies to pitch. It did change over time, as everybody soon had a PR company representing them. But we took pride in interviewing people with whom we made our own direct connections. I spent over a year trying to land interviews with Laurent X and Manuel Göttsching."

My own experience closely mirrors Robby's. I was initially a staff writer, but while I didn't become picture editor, I eventually became Assistant Editor, editing all the reviews pages, which appealed to my analytical mind, and licensing the music for the physical cover-mount CDs with Roy Carr in the main IPC building. My first-ever interview for the magazine was with Monsieur Bob Sinclar (appropriate and fantastique since we mostly discussed his single *Gym Tonic* with Thomas Bangalter), and well before I became a full-time member of staff, I would be chatting to Daft Punk, Carl Cox, Goldie, and Hybrid about their artistry at the Muzik Awards. The summer just before I joined full time, I spoke to Roger Sanchez and Pet Shop Boy Chris Lowe about Creamfields and rave, before diving back into the pool myself via Pacha, Space, Privilege, and Bora Bora. In many ways, it was my finishing school and training for a better future. My IPC days started around 10:30 a.m. and finished when they finished, which was often around 9 p.m. or even 2 a.m. if it was a Thursday and there was a trip to The AKA Bar ahead.

Back to da Bank: "I like to think I was first in and last out… even if I was out with Ben at the Met Bar the night before! I just loved being there. Hearing who had left a message on your answerphone because you were talking to the A-Z of dance music every week. To be thrust into that was mind-blowing."

Push, however, didn't see himself staying for the duration.

"As I mentioned earlier, *Muzik* was HUGE for me. The way Ben and I worked was interesting. Ben was more feet on the ground, going out every night and knew everybody. I wanted to steer and guide it in terms of the writing. So Ben was in charge of the music and I was in charge of the writing. We couldn't have done it without each other. I left *Melody Maker* in 1994, we launched in May 1995, and I left in 1998: issue 42 or 43 was my last one. I was utterly exhausted and there had been no sleep for weeks with such a hard slog—it was always a slog—and I remember once I got on the train and thought if I could survive until issue 40, that would be it for me. And weirdly, I left around issue 43. I wasn't sure if I needed it or if it needed me. That was partly my age. I wanted to do something else. I wasn't bored, but I felt like I needed a change. I had another idea for a magazine that IPC didn't do. And I still believed in this idea and wanted to take it somewhere else. They gave me a few months' wages to go, but there was lots going on. And my memory is that Ben was about to go or had one foot out the door, and we brought in Frank Tope. We offered him a job, and for a while, a bunch of things came together. Robby was also on board. I was 37. 40 would come quickly, and I needed to have a midlife crisis! But the one thing was I was offered a book deal and did a book on E that came out, so as well as a pay-off, I had a bit of money from Omnibus."

And so, he left! Ben then took full control until issue 57 before launching his entrepreneurial career, becoming artist manager for Richie Hawtin, Rob da Bank (for over 15 years), and many other influential electronic acts. His relationships from the *Muzik* days live on through his IMS Ibiza (International Music Summit) platform with Pete Tong and Danny Whittle, and creating the global trade body for electronic music called the Association for Electronic Music. He is still fighting the good fight and holds on to that same little brown Filofax he used to guard with his life, which had the personal contacts of everybody from Carl Craig to Chris Lowe to Daddy G from Massive Attack.

CHAPTER SIX: MUZIK IS THE ANSWER

Which brings us back to Robby, who, like Frank Tope, was now full-time. When we spoke for this book, I reminded Robby of the Ibiza da Bank feature, which involved him running around the island on a strict IPC budget.

"I think that might have been my first proper feature, and Ben had the wisdom to send me with Jamie B, my brother in misadventure. It was the first time I went to see José Padilla at Café Del Mar, and it totally awoke something in me. And I like that Ben was serious about his work and craft but let my slightly fun side come out. But Ibiza did nearly kill me eventually. We lived in a shitty apartment above The Mezzanine Bar, and I was usually stranded outside. I got myself in a tangle in Ibiza. Ibiza had many high points, but I hit it as Manumission was peaking, and at this point, the clubs editor or any editor was wined and dined and given anything they wanted. So the main club editor or anyone from *Muzik* in Ibiza—i.e., me—was fully VIPed for weeks on end, and it took its toll. Fond memories!"

I, too, would spend five or six weeks on and off on the island that summer, listening to an endless stream of immaculate house music and meeting clubbers of every colour of the spectrum. It was like being thrown into a swimming pool: you either sank or you swam, and thankfully, we both survived the experience and lived to tell this tale. But in 1999, I didn't have a huge amount of confidence in my writing, and it appears that Robby felt the same way. "I don't think I am the greatest writer, but at *Muzik*, I was first in and last out. I was a team player and 100% committed to the cause. I did a fair amount of features, and being the club editor meant things like going down to review Fatboy Slim at a Scout Hut in Brighton… he was barely Fatboy and playing a scout hut with a freezer at the back. He'd open it up and start throwing frozen cod around the room. And then I got mugged on the way home, which was memorable, but he's been a lifelong friend since. I went to Miami and New York, and Basement Jaxx were playing at Twilo, a legendary NYC club, and I was meeting DJ Sneak and David Morales, and that was totally mind-blowingly cool."

Like me, Rob da Bank is aware that for many years, *Muzik* was indeed the answer. I started writing for *Muzik* in 1998 and was there until IPC finally closed its doors in 2003. By this point, pretty much everyone else mentioned above, beyond the odd freelancer, had moved on. The magazine closed midway through issue 99. "Out of all the things I've done... selfishly, I think there were points where I was a journalist, I had a festival, and I was a resident on Radio 1, and *Muzik* was at the centre of all of those spokes," says Robby.

Our chat ends with a statement from da Bank I completely agree with for myself: "I still have the dream life."

CHAPTER SEVEN
The End Is the Beginning Is the End

It must be obvious that I am incredibly proud of the work we did at *Muzik*.

Although I took full-time employment in September 1999, I had been working behind the scenes for a good eighteen months already. That meant interviewing people like Daft Punk and Goldie at the annual *Muzik* Awards, observing how dance music was starting to attract superstar guests like Kate Moss and Noel Gallagher, and finding time to dance to peeps like Trevor Nelson up close and personal once the (not-so-hard) work was done. The 1999 awards featured after-party sets from Trevor, Carl Cox, Judge Jules, Danny Rampling, and Roger Sanchez, which again shows you how much clout *Muzik* magazine had at this point: I always called them the dance music Oscars, and with good reason. Always the hottest ticket in town, this was the only place that anyone working in dance music would congregate annually, and it was not only glamorous and glitzy but also wonderful to watch. I bought a brand-new suit in Brighton for £400 – a small fortune for me back then – in honour of the awards and wore that same suit to The End for the after-party. It was worth every penny.

I was now living on my own in Leyton, and while there wasn't much to explore beyond the local park, what I now had was a full-time wage, and I honestly felt like the king of my own East London castle. Now on a full-time salary of £17,500 plus expenses (God, I miss magazine expenses), I could finally afford to buy Very Nice Things once in a while. These, for the most part, would be the latest Nike trainers and new white t-shirts to wear to the best parties in town. I even took out an IPC pension, and let me tell you, it was the smartest future decision 25-year-old me ever, ever took.

Still edited by Ben Turner, the next issue of *Muzik* to arrive featured the undisputed, number-one 90s superstar DJ Paul Oakenfold and was written by future (temporary) editor Dave Fowler, a hedonistic night creature who was somewhat overfond of nighttime temptations and had more issues than Vogue, with none of that magazine's inner or outer sparkle. Dave is probably the only person in this book who has since disappeared from the face of the earth, but to be fair, he did an OK job with this Oakenfold cover feature, albeit in his usual bombastic writing style. (He also got Judge Jules horribly drunk before Jules' own cover feature with *Muzik* the year before: "Unethical journalism to say the least," is how Jules described it to me recently. "Although, to be fair, I was a willing recipient!")

The reason for Paul's second *Muzik* cover (which featured Paul Oakenfold in the back of an open-top 4X4 with 'HOME' in capitals on the licence plate) was simple: he was the headline-grabbing resident of that shiny new club in Leicester Square called home (with a lowercase 'h') alongside Birmingham/Space Ibiza DJ and producer Steve Lawler, a very young Jacques Lu Cont, and, very occasionally, the NYC DJ legend Danny Tenaglia. Darren Hughes, the former promoter of home at Space and originally the co-promoter and founder of Liverpool's Cream brand with James Barton, was the man behind this short-lived club venture and the often-quality bookings. However, dance music PR Ed Cartwright remembers losing out on a Leftfield cover at the last minute when Paul was bumped to a cover around the club's opening. Fabric had stalled at the last minute and didn't open until later in the year, giving home the advantage in the press with publications like *Muzik*, who recognised that Oakenfold in '99 had the same success level and profile as a star footballer does today. Editor Ben Turner had made his decision, and I'm pretty sure that he still stands by it.

With honorary shouts to *Disco Pogo*, the one thing that's changed since *Mixmag* closed its UK magazine over lockdown in 2020 is not only a quality publication that covered the world's dance music and clubbing agenda top to bottom, but also, before you even get to the inside – cover lines.

Let's look at the Paul Oakenfold cover.

"21 clubs for the 21st century"

"Leftfield – return of the originals"

"Groove Armada, Death In Vegas, Aphex Twin, Renaissance"

And the biggest one:

"Oakenfold – The world's biggest DJ comes home to save London clubland"

Ironically, this was quite tame to some of the magazine's more 'out there' cover lines over at *Mixmag* or *DJ Mag*.

My favourite part was always the spurious ones: in the corner, if you weren't paying attention, there is one more in yellow:

"Special issue"

No screaming exclamation mark, but equally no real justification. How is this issue special or different? There is no CD attached to it, no free poster, or promise of a free packet of Shreddies if you collect six tokens. But "Special issue" very much sums up the spirit of the dance magazine age in the late nineties. In other words, PLEASE BUY THIS VERY SPECIAL ISSUE, IT MAY CHANGE YOUR LIFE!

Inside, there was the usual mirth and mayhem. Mike Manumission was asked his favourite sexual position (it was late '99, so by this point, *Muzik* was chasing *Mixmag* for the same ABCs, if not the same STDs) and one of the best Double Eggs appeared in the corner of the same page. Under a photo of Sharam from Deep Dish, the words "David Baddiel," and under a photo of David Baddiel, "Sharam, Deep Dish."

'Uppers and Downers' was another must-read every month, even if it was a nod to Boys Own's similar column. In this issue, we had the quintessential *Muzik* choice at the top of Uppers: "The sunset at Café Del Mar – better than the eclipse any day. 2,000 people clapping the sun," and Euros (the ecstasy pill du jour at the time) – "currently the real single currency in Ibiza, if you know what we mean."

There's also a piece on a new band called Lemon Jelly, which was penned by our resident Balearic chill expert Rob Da Bank.

CHAPTER SEVEN: THE END IS THE BEGINNING IS THE END

Never let it be said that *Muzik* didn't possess the best ears in the business. "At Impotent Fury we go from painfully naff to painfully trendy with everything in between," said Fred Deakin from Lemon Jelly, also summing up *Muzik*'s own attitude to the best party soundtracks, at least the ones that happened in my house. "House music gets you going, but it gets you going more if you've just had 30 minutes of British comedy hits. The relief makes it more special." Robby had much in common with Gilles Peterson: both expert selectors rather than the best DJs in the business. Tellingly, Gilles is quoted in the piece, discussing Lemon Jelly's song *Homage To Patagonia* as being "the new sound of worldwide music." There's a future FM radio station name in there somewhere.

And we can't forget the cover feature, which Dave Fowler, for once, reined in. "London is the centre of the world when it comes to music. We all know the north is better than the south," said Paul, selling himself and the club to the same savvy audience. "That's why I want to make home like a northern club."

At the end of the piece, Paul is asked his favourite five restaurants in the world, and these include The Oriental in Bangkok, The Four Seasons in Bali, The Grand Hyatt in Shanghai, West hotels, and The Armand chain, "13 hotels in America, all with great service."

But *Muzik* knew it still had to balance, which is why, beyond the Balearic bullshit and the features on Argentina and a returning Leftfield, there was also a typically excellent two-page feature by Dorian Lynskey with the day's underground darlings, Death In Vegas. "Big beat was a shitty stick we were tarnished with from day one," says Richard Fearless as his opening gambit in the piece. "It became like Jive Bunny after a while; hideous, hideous music. This album is a rejection of that." And Andy Crysell's five-star review of their debut album *The Contino Sessions* backed up that assertion, saying "only the certifiably mental can be happy all of the time." It was an album that opened with the foreboding *Dirge* by Fearless, featuring his then-girlfriend, the former singer of One Dove, Dot Allison. The second track, *Soul Auctioneer*, features Primal Scream's lead singer Bobby Gillespie, which makes the album just about as Heavenly as it can get.

You can draw a through line from Paul Oakenfold to the major DJ players of yesterday and today, and that would include Tiësto, Paul Van Dyk, Diplo, Armin Van Buuren, and David Guetta. All showmen, sure, but most importantly, all of them with their eye on the prize and the best presidential suite money can buy. It's the precise opposite of Weatherall, who refused to play snakes and ladders on the circuit to success, and today's fees would roll their eyes at how far they've come since going (back) home in '99.

But *Muzik* had other issues more close to, well, home.

Calvin Bush was a sudden shock departure after my incredible summer in Space, and that resulted in a major office reshuffle. Robby was promoted from Clubs Editor, Frank Tope was in the main editorial hot seat adjacent to me as Deputy Editor, and former editorial assistant Karen Young was moved up to Club Editor. Ben Turner was roving around to an insane degree, which meant that Frank was in charge of the magazine's overall schedule day-to-day. I was in the corner next to Robby with more free music than I'd ever experienced in my life, and every day, people like Caroline Prothero at Virgin Records would bike us their latest white labels or promo CDs, which we devoured hungrily as they arrived almost gift-wrapped at Hatfield House. I had a cute Apple Mac computer, a Lauryn Hill mouse mat, my trusty blue glasses (which always steamed up under pressure), and could finally afford a decent mid-range wardrobe, which was offset by the odd promo t-shirt from Soma Recordings or another similar electronic imprint. *Muzik* felt fresh and exciting.

My hairdresser of choice was called Hair By Fairy in Covent Garden, which is somehow still there today, tucked away in Neal's Yard. It was a Robby suggestion one afternoon, even though Rob's own tonsorial stylings were always arguably rather questionable. I felt right at home, which really was wonderful. Another da Bank suggestion, as I found my feet, was the new David Lynch movie *The Straight Story*, which I dutifully took myself to see at a tiny cinema in Leicester Square that's long since departed. It's a movie about an old man who makes a long journey by lawnmower to see his brother, and it's one of my all-time favourite films of the era; the music is also incredible.

Each and every day, we had access to the very heart of the industry via email and phone, and our landlines would ring merrily every few minutes with calls from people like Anna Goodman from Abstrakt PR or DJ Paulette at Azuli, asking if we'd listened to the Knee Deep remixes of Afro Medusa's 'Pasilda'. (Reader, we had, and I still listen to it regularly.) Being the youngest on the team, I was the route of least resistance, and I didn't like leaving my phone on answer phone too often, so soon I'd started forging friendships with all the major label spokespeople and the occasional promoter inviting us to events. Rich McGinnis (later behind The Warehouse Project but then working at Chibuku) was reportedly instructed to treat Karen Young and me with caution until he realised that we were essentially on the same team. But Karen's path is also worth mentioning, and since we also spent an hour reminiscing about her role at Muzik and her life before and after her time at the title, I'm going to pause my own thoughts and hand over the proverbial microphone to her.

"*Muzik* changed my life," says Karen simply, looking back on the publication a cool quarter-century later from her current home in Mexico. Now living and working in Tulum, running her fusion restaurant called WILD, Karen shared the same ethos as myself, Robby, Frank, and Ben: work hard, play harder – but always make sure you deliver your copy on time. "Picking up the first edition of the magazine in 1995, we went to a party in Portugal based on that," she remembers. "My first encounter with Ben Turner was when my best friend Jo and I had bought the first issue of *Muzik*, where it states 'Lisbon – the new Ibiza' (Ben did that 'new Ibiza' a lot after that), and she said 'Let's go!' – and so we did. 'A Paradise Called Portugal' was *Muzik*'s week-long collaboration with Tribal UK, local promoters KAOS, and international DJs, and the first party was in Kremlin, Lisbon. That's where we met Ben and Adrian (the photographer Raize-A-Head) and we stuck with them for the rest of the tour. Kenny Hawkes, Luke Solomon, Phil Perry, Miles Holloway, Scott Shindig, Phil Mison, to Danny Tenaglia and Laurent Garnier were all there DJing in various venues, and we got a very long train journey hungover to the big KAOS rave in a castle (Castillo de Montemor-o-Velho), stayed there until after the sun rose, and then all ended up crashing in the same hotel room. From there, a long-standing friendship was born. I recall that year, Ben and

CHAPTER SEVEN: THE END IS THE BEGINNING IS THE END

I had a joint birthday party at The Velvet Rooms with Laurent Garnier doing an epic 8-hour set." "I was still at university at the time, buying *Muzik* religiously every month, partying religiously every weekend to their recommendations, buying records they recommended, and playing those records at the university disco. *Muzik* was my bible. After graduating, my first job was with Virgin Records in the marketing department as a junior marketing assistant, and from there, I went to Deconstruction at BMG. I was PA to the two MDs at Deconstruction, Pete Hadfield and Keith Blackhurst, and James Barton was A&R at the time there. One day, Ben came in to see Barton and told me there was an opening at the magazine and would I like to be poached. I didn't hesitate. At Deconstruction, despite the great label and great times, I remember Keith shouting throughout the day, 'Oi Karen, what comes between 'S' and 'U'?' He liked to drink a lot of tea, and frankly, I was never going to be just a tea girl, so it was time to move on. Working at *Muzik* was not only a dream come true but the beginning of the best times of my career."

Karen remembers her time at the magazine as one that involved more club nights than were sensible, and I certainly remember visiting a whole ton of clubs and festivals with her and various members of the team. Ultimate B.A.S.E. with Carl Cox was an early favourite (at The Velvet Rooms in Charing Cross). "I was going to Ultimate B.A.S.E., Turnmills, Heaven, Plastic People and THEN The End, fabric, and home, a couple of hours of sleep if I was lucky, and back to the office. I was privileged to spend weeks in Ibiza every summer, Miami Winter Music Conferences every year, travel to Mexico to review the ACA World Sound Festival, and I was the first UK journalist to review Exit Festival. That was due to *Muzik*'s Bedroom Bedlam tours. From there, they asked me to help them book and promote the festival, and as it stood out as one of the best I had ever been to, I leapt at that and went out on my own. Exit Festival was my baby for the next 15 years. Working at *Muzik* and after *Muzik* was the best time of my life."

Happily, Karen's experience in the *Muzik* office was, for the most part, extremely positive, even though the only three women working full time were Karen, picture editor Julie Bentley, and a tough, no-nonsense production editor called Lindsey McWhinnie. "Before Ben poached me, my first job was with Virgin Records in the marketing department as a junior marketing assistant, and from there, I went to BMG/Deconstruction. It was a male-dominated industry. As women, we had to work harder and we didn't get the acknowledgement from managers to agents. But I must say this: working at *Muzik* was the best time of my life."

If you're wondering what happened to home, well, back in 2001, it was closed by Westminster Council late in March due to alleged evidence of open drug-dealing occurring within the club, despite its famously tough door checks. The club went into receivership shortly after it was closed, became Vertigo, then later The Penthouse, and most recently, a branch of Greggs. But home's loss in Leicester Square was beneficial to The End and fabric, who could now access some of the bigger talent that Darren Hughes and later Paul Barkworth were almost certainly booking exclusively before. We should have seen the signs early on, though; it was like opening a branch of Dior Homme in the middle of Leyton High Street.

At The End, we'd all bond with the team behind the scenes. That included Layo Paskin and his sister Zoe, as well as the club's amazing back-end staff, such as the irrepressible and whip-smart

CHAPTER SEVEN: THE END IS THE BEGINNING IS THE END

Liam O'Hare, who was General Manager from the day it opened until the day it closed, and DJ agent Charlotte Schilcher. In many ways, we felt that the club's underground ethos matched our own left-leaning musical sentiments. At The End, time had no meaning, and we would often be the last ones standing as the music ground to a halt around 8 a.m. I remember an epic set from Deep Dish—it was an incredible night from start to finish—and Cassius did the same for my brain in this exact era.

It was the same at fabric. I was there on opening night in October 1999 and have been dancing to the same beat every season since. Early nights were promoted by Steve Blonde and later by Shaun Roberts, who was so cruelly taken from us by colon cancer, despite a record-breaking charity event to raise funds for his care. [1] One event with Carl Cox and Matthew B stays with me to this day—and, of course, I was there when Daft Punk performed in November 1999. Like me, resident Craig Richards also celebrates 25 years within those hallowed walls this year.

Even though the club is no longer in the hands of original owner Keith Reilly, its fiercely underground ethos remains strong, thanks to a team that includes programming director Judy Griffith, who has been at the heart of fabric since its inception in 1999. A true legend of the industry, Judy has no intention of going anywhere.

It says a lot that fabric is the only one of the brilliant late-night dens still standing as a going concern. The End is now

---

1 (Shaun passed away on Christmas Eve 2022 after being diagnosed with colon cancer in 2019 but is never far from our thoughts and his wake in Hackney was one of the most moving events I've ever experienced.)

resolutely empty despite being sold 15 years ago to be turned into flats—though those iconic blue walls mostly remain. Liam showed me around the venue four or five years ago, and it's all still there, just with the addition of memories and pools of water that refuse to shift.

To its eternal credit, fabric (always a lowercase "f") has been a uniquely single-minded institution from the start. Selling out musically was never part of its agenda, even as the surrounding area began to gentrify. Even the building itself—a multi-level Victorian space that once served as a butchers' market and storage facility—hasn't changed much beyond the occasional sonic tweak and the addition of a new smoking area.

The men originally behind it were the always-intense Keith Reilly and Cameron Leslie. Like Judy, Leslie is still there today. The sound system, especially in Room 1, is truly one of a kind and has been continuously refined over the years.

Globally, fabric has become synonymous with a high-quality, cutting-edge club experience. Reilly himself still treasures the night John Peel played at the club in February 2002. The accompanying mix CD, which memorably includes Peel's all-time favourite, *Teenage Kicks* by The Undertones, remains an essential piece of club history. [2]

I worked on a free fanzine for The End with Ben Turner and several of the club's key personnel around this time. As usual, I

---

[2] I have most of the fabric mixes on CD and they are a reminder of a time and a place where tech-house meant Terry Francis and Jon Marsh from 90s crossover dance act The Beloved, both of whom delivered classic early (or should that be late night?) mixes for the series.

kept two copies (for the sake of my sanity, some of the items I kept two of have recently been downgraded to one).

The booklet, the size of a typical football program, featured not only interviews with Mr. C of *The Shamen*—the face and underground spirit of the club—but also emerging artists like Erol Alkan, who ran his club night *Trash* there for many years, and NYC legend Danny Tenaglia.

In a section called *True Players*, the booklet went behind the scenes to spotlight the unsung heroes—the people who made things happen but rarely received the same accolades as the talent. The End boasted some of the best people in the industry, much like the original team at *Muzik*. Unsurprisingly, many of these individuals have gone on to significant roles in the music industry, including Ty Vigrass, Ajay Jayaram, and Liam O'Hare.

"Before I joined The End, I was running squat parties and a restaurant," Liam recalls in the booklet. "When this job came up, I could at last combine my two passions! We've never compromised at the club, musically or artistically. I really don't think we've hit our pinnacle—I'd love to be here in 2015!"

We must also give credit to Claudia Nicholson, Promotions Manager from 1995 to 2000. "It was an exciting time musically, especially with drum 'n' bass and breakbeat," she recalls. "We were quite snobby about the music, really, but I'm glad The End never sold out."

I also spoke to the infamous industry agent David Levy—now representing the likes of Fatboy Slim and Madness but then at ITB—about the club. He had this to say:

"I know what they've been through to survive, and the lack of compromise in standards is all the more remarkable for that.

I'm thrilled that, in the next decade, one of my favourite clients, Timo Maas, is going to be a resident there. Matt and Layo are our clients. London is all about clubs like The End—adventurous, multi-layered, and always about the party. They make a mean cocktail in AKA too!"

Mr. C and Danny Tenaglia also shared their distinctive perspectives.

When I asked Richard West, aka Mr. C of *The Shamen*, about the importance of The End, he said:

"The End has been a catalyst for electronic music. If it wasn't for The End, I don't think the world would be where it is today. When we started, there was nowhere to go! We gave producers a place to play music—the club was a springboard. It gave Americans like Derrick Carter a place to play. From Frankie Knuckles to Deep Dish, The End showed this could be done without hype or over-marketing. It was serious music. And people loved it!"

We also reminisced about a party in 1999, one where I drunkenly approached Daft Punk after their set at El Divino on the White Isle.

"The End held a series of memorable parties at El Divino," Mr. C continued. "We had Sneak, Daft Punk, myself, and Derrick Carter. It was good but only half full! But nobody succeeds in Ibiza in their first season."

Danny Tenaglia described The End as something of a rebirth for him.

"My performance at AKA came at a time when the true meaning and passion for what I do had started to dwindle as my career—and that of so many peers—took a 'global' direction. It started to feel impossible to do small events where people came solely for the music. I remember the intimacy at AKA feeling similar to playing for Phil Perry at Full Circle, JBO at Sub Station South, Back to Basics, or Ultimate B.A.S.E. with Carl Cox and Jim Masters. I miss those days.

The End was an incredible venue—truly a back-to-basics approach. I remember playing classics like *Casa De X* by Deep Dish and BT on Tribal Records. Major respect to everyone at The End for maintaining a vibe that's consistent and authentic!"

Tiga offered a perspective on the club's indie-dance element, which I loved as much as the 4/4 beats I was imbibing in Ibiza.

"I vaguely remember hearing about The End in a dance music magazine," he started, likely referring to *Muzik*. "When I finally had my chance to *Move Any Mountain*, I was ready! I played *Giant* by The The as my last song, but I pitched it too fast, and it sounded pretty weird. Actually, one strange memory comes to mind—I remember it being the first night in my life I felt older. Fitting. The End."

As this club-focused chapter comes to a close, I'll give the final word to Karen Young, who summed up this unbelievably exciting electronic era beautifully:

"I really believe that the whole industry was on the same team. With *Muzik*, we were purists. Artists and people who worked in clubs like AKA were all having a great time together. There wasn't much pretentiousness—though the odd issue arose, like when fabric pulled ads after Keith Reilly disliked a review—but we had the best time, travelling to different places alongside the punters and promoters. It was a time when people made lifelong partners and friends—that was the clubbing culture. It was always full of love. How much fun did we have!"

We had it all—and then we had it again. We were an incredible team, one that remains invisibly bound together by club walls and sticky floors to this day.

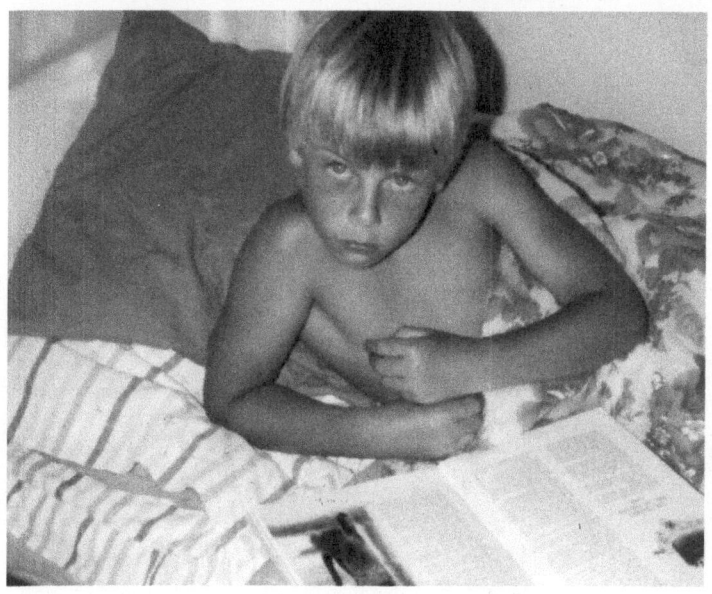

The expression of a boy who's just been interrupted from reading.

Me with my beloved Transformer toy Metroplex back in Burgess Hill.

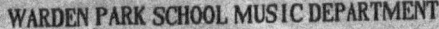

I still can't believe I kept this 'Elijah And The Baal Gang' flyer from 1988!

Fast-forward to Haywards Heath College, where I played Prince and Simply Red in the common room every single day in 1992.

Another find from Mum's loft: the One Dove photo that accompanied my first full page feature in The Warwick Boar back in '93. Weatherall vibes.

My sister's N1 clan: with Danny, Antonella, Cherelle and Hayden Thomas.

Early '94 with my Warden Park school friend Steve to my left and Rich from my corridor far-left. Note The Utah Saints tour poster on the wall!

Young love: Anna and I in my Cryfields Hall dorm mid '94 surrounded by all my favourite rock and dance iconography.

In an era before social media, I am so glad I asked someone to take a photo of me in my Manumission uniform at Privilege: 1999.

"Deal with it, Richmond!" Roger and Junior Sanchez (no relation) at the Muzik Awards, 2000. I imagine my brain had already clocked that these two had recently remixed Daft Punk's 'Revolution 909'.

Sasha's Miami boat parties at WMC (Winter Music Conference) in the early 2000s were the stuff of legend. As a DJ, he remains the very definition of consistent!

"Smurf!" I took this ace photo of producer Brian 'BT' Transeau and friend at Amnesia one Thursday night for Cream.

Muzik's Karen Young and friend at DC10, circa 2000: squint a bit and you'll see Danny Tenaglia in the DJ booth at the back.

Another shot I'm so happy to have captured: Jo Mills and Charlie Chester at DC10, when it really was the wild west.

Mel C's Es Paradis video shoot invite, 2000! Remember being given this on Bora Bora. Ibiza's most famous foam club, in San An at least.

The 2001 Muzik Awards with (y)our host Pete Tong. Laurent Garnier and Wookie both performed live that year, as did an impromptu Sophie Ellis-Bextor.

Not sure why I took this photo of Norman Cook's Pacha Buenos Aires vinyl set up but it definitely captures a moment in time.

Pretty sure my friend Helen took this: the final Muzik team press trip to see Eminem at Milton Keynes Bowl in '03. A brilliant day out.

More Circo Loco, this time after the mid 2000s red wall rebrand with my trusty number cruncher and bass lover Yvette Redmond in the middle, Lorna to the left and Charlie Mayhew to the right.

Myself and Russell Davis pondering life over a curry in Soho: I really don't know where my life would have ended up if we hadn't traipsed to Tribal Gathering together.

Another great shot taken by yours truly of Nile Rodgers, Fiora Cutler and Marco Niemerski behind the scenes of the Tensnake video 'Love Sublime'.

I went to every single Bestival without fail when it was on the Isle Of Wight: this picture I took one Sunday may help to explain why.

Bringing things more up to date, IMS 2018 with my friend Taryn Ross, who runs the Urban Junkies site: "what's happening?"

This was at Tom March and Nancy's epic wedding and features a few familiar London faces, including the much-missed fabric promoter Shaun Roberts.

Closing out the On Tour photo album with a vintage shot of my Mum: Celia Ann Moore, R.I.P.

CHAPTER EIGHT
TINY DANCER

My mum once tried to get me to learn Latin after school when I was 11, but I just wasn't having it. Unlike English, French, or German, it felt like a seriously dead language to me. If there was one thing that mattered to me, it was where things were going next.

One thing was clear, however: things at *Muzik* started to unravel after Ben left, followed by Frank. By this point, Karen Young from *Muzik* had given me a pen name: "Raving Ralph." I wouldn't be surprised if I'm still saved in her burner phone under that moniker.

I was still having all the fun in the world, but I don't think I was editor material at 25 or 26 — and *Muzik* went through a series of editors that the world has (thankfully) long forgotten.

There was Dave Fowler, a lifelong Turnmills white-trance fan who somehow balanced being *Muzik*'s boss with a membership to Sundays at DJ Tall Paul's club in Farringdon (which, like The End, was sold long ago and turned into flats). Dave faced the chop after a series of ill-informed editorial decisions that, despite his initial pitch, didn't help magazine sales at all. Dave was replaced by an amiable but sadly musically inept Scottish character called Chris Elwell-Sutton, who, like Dave, had promised IPC that sales would increase under his tenure, even though they resolutely did not. (And if you're wondering what happened to Chris, he is now "a data privacy specialist providing strategic legal counsel to clients in financial services," which might explain what endeared him to the suits at IPC in the early 2000s.)

Chris, as you might have guessed, didn't last long either, which meant it was the turn of former *Top Gear* magazine editor Conor McNicholas—a man with his eye on a higher prize (namely, *NME*). Conor plotted his route to the indie-inkie top via a stint at *Muzik* while it was still based at Hatfield House.

To be fair to Conor, he did a much better job than either Dave or Chris. The relaunched issue, featuring Tom and Ed Chemical and a CD mix licensed by yours truly that included their classic single *Superstylin'*, sold considerably better than any issue from the previous 12 months under the new redesign. But looking back, you can sense the ambition.

As for me, I just watched all of this unfold from the sidelines and tried to make myself invaluable. That was my biggest lesson of this era: keep your head down, keep your spirits up, and keep track of where the industry and the constant stream of music were going. It was a simple ethos, powered by a lot of caffeine and (power/pub) lunches, but it was the one I had to follow religiously at 26.

But now, the lines were being blurred to a point where it was impossible to know where work ended and the real fun began. Was going to Miami for a week actual work, or was it the biggest music blowout on the planet? Was hanging out with our favourite artists until stupid o'clock part of the editorial job, or merely a perk of the position? All I know is that there are people we all met back then—Carl Cox, Paul Woolford, Yousef, Lottie, FC Kahuna, Lee Burridge, Craig Richards, Sasha (AKA the original Tyrant), and countless others—who are still only the touch of a button away today. I bumped into Muzik's former breaks editor, Tayo, at Hackney Central station the week before writing this chapter, not unlike my recent encounter on the same road a few weeks earlier with Shane O'Neill. These moments serve as reminders of what a special time we all had on the road to Patagonia.

Once Dave Fowler was made editor over Frank Tope, it wasn't long before Frank departed for a more promising freelance career. Frank's taste and style are the very definition of "across the board," but I have yet to find a bigger trainspotter in his field, apart from perhaps British writer and equally esteemed DJ, Bill Brewster. Today, Frank is a DJ, artist manager, and A&R consultant (not unlike myself), but it was Frank's kindness and ability to keep *Muzik* balanced after Ben Turner left that made him the magazine's biggest unsung hero during its middle years. But that could equally be because, unlike, say, Tayo and Adam Freeland, who definitely harboured ambitions of being a rock star, Frank has remained a humble, behind-the-scenes kind of character.

Unlike me, Rob da Bank officially left Muzik early in 2000 (side note: IPC tried everything to get him to stay on, and they just couldn't manage it). The next thing we knew, he'd started a brand new event called Bestival on the Isle of Wight, where he now lives with his wife Josie and their family, becoming the island's unofficial music mayor. Over the years, his impeccable electronic, rock, and pop bookings went from Mylo, Basement Jaxx, and Fatboy Slim in year one, to Kraftwerk, The Beastie

Boys, Nile Rodgers, and ultimately Elton John. The crowd grew from 5,000 punters initially to at least ten times that. Not too shabby is an apt way to describe that leap in life.

So, while Tayo was continually late delivering his breakbeat copy (and I probably lost a good week of my life endlessly chasing it—even to Sydney, Australia, in '02), Frank was keeping an eye on the new album from Basement Jaxx and neo-soul nuggets from Jill Scott to Rawkus-signed hip hop from the likes of Mos Def and Pharoahe Monch. I'm not sure I could have had a better human being to sit across from and learn from. He was also able to keep Rob da Bank in check better than anyone else, including his future manager, Ben Turner.

Frank was aware that while we were essentially living in a dance publication laboratory, we still had a proper job to do and, more importantly, a publisher to appease. So, while the original first 50 issues of *Muzik* had stayed on the more underground tip (and only *Muzik* in the mid-90s would have dared to run covers with Basement Jaxx and a lion, or a solo Grooverider—"THIS is hardcore," what a great cover line), after Ben left (and even before), there was genuine pressure to boost circulation. And thus, we entered a different era of *Muzik*, one where we would occasionally put a girl with no name or number on the cover, or sneak in a cover mix from someone like Paul Van Dyk. That Sasha *Muzik* cover I mentioned earlier summed up this new ethos brilliantly: the cover, a gatefold, features Sasha and Lottie, but the CD mix attached to it was pure PVD. As the club kids say today... we move.

The 50th issue of *Muzik* was celebrated at Heaven on Villiers Street in Charing Cross with a pitch-perfect line-up that summed up the ethos of the era. *Muzik* and Bedrock were the hosts, John Digweed was the headliner as the main Bedrock resident, and the line-up featured Grooverider, Basement Jaxx, Darren Emerson, Carl Cox, Danny Howells, and Sasha. Everyone played for peanuts.

"They had a really strong audience," remembers Frank of *Muzik*'s glory days.

"Bedroom DJs—in the DJ community, you will still get people who say they loved *Muzik* because it spoke directly to them. *Mixmag* had a less cohesive audience: a lot more clubbers bought it because they wanted to know where they should go on a Saturday night."

Given that this story is as much about the people behind the publications as the bigger brand itself, it's only right that we let Frank 'Dope' Tope tell his backstory for a moment.

"I started off freelancing for *DJ Magazine* when Chris Coco was the editor," says Frank, who remains as enthusiastic about his role as a (house) music champion as ever. "I'd written for my university magazine, and we did a night in 1991 where we did a theatre-style programme. (Original Boys Own DJ) Terry Farley thought that was good, so I ended up writing a piece for Boys Own that eventually came out. Having a few ideas and having Boys Own as a calling card, and having been to the Zap acid house nights in '88 in Brighton where Chris was playing, made me feel like I could approach DJs."

Andy Pemberton was the man who brought him into *Mixmag*. A brilliant writer who had previously edited the rock-centric *Q Magazine* in London and launched the excellent *Blender* in New York, Frank remains grateful for the early editorial support—which was not unlike the one I was later granted myself. "Andy brought me in to freelance for *Mixmag*, and then they got me to help collate the charts every week for *Mixmag Update*. Bill [Brewster] would meet me and drive me to Slough to the DMC headquarters. And then Bill left to run DMC in New York, and I was offered a full-time position to run *Update* and the music section of *Mixmag*. I was working half out of Slough and half out of the *MM* office, working with Tony and Christine Prince. They brought *Update* into *Mixmag* and had a team working with me who also worked on *Mixmag*—Andy Taylor, the graphic designer, and Sarah Foote after him, and they're both still in dance music. Nick Jones was one of the main *Mixmag* freelance writers. *Update* came out every week as a kind of parish newsletter for dance music. It seemed a pain to produce every week, but talking to the DJs now, I realise it was quite a big thing for them. At *Mixmag*, I was the resident music head and the musical trainspotter. I was there for two years, which, when you're in your fifties, seems short!"

"Looking at *Mixmag*, you've got this huge explosion of post-acid house '90s culture, and that was a big spectrum," says Frank, whose passionate, trainspotter-driven perspective is crucial to this era and therefore this book. "Bedroom DJs through to casual Saturday night clubbers, and the clubbers went from techno and d'n'b through to the shiny shirt and fluffy bra glam clubbing that was exploding across the country—club brands like Cream, Golden, Chuff Chuff, and Miss Moneypennys in Birmingham. *Mixmag* was the market leader, but the strength and the weakness of that was it was trying to be all things for everybody. The focus was on clubbers, and that gave *Muzik* room to appeal to music fans. And equally, you could say it also left room to have a magazine aimed almost completely at the casual clubber. Then *Ministry* [magazine] came along, removed the musical content almost completely, and aimed entirely at the casual clubber. It didn't seem to believe in anything, which is maybe why it didn't work."

It was around this time that the hedonistic former *Muzik* writer and editor, Dave Fowler, offered me £30K to leave *Muzik* and move to *Ministry* down in Elephant and Castle, which, as Frank rightly remembers, was by far the worst dance magazine in the market: as if I would have left the Premier League! (But I did come back and tell the IPC suits and got a pay rise. *Ministry Magazine*, which rarely put artists on the cover, sputtered out and was closed by Ministry of Sound bosses in 2002.)

This is how the story was broken by the baby version of *The Guardian* website in '02:

"Ministry of Sound, the embattled dance music brand that turned a South London club into a music, publishing, and clothing empire, is closing its flagship magazine. Staff were told today that the December issue of *Ministry* would be the last, although the company plans to launch another magazine to replace it early next year. Ministry of Sound is thought to be under pressure to cut costs from investor 3i, the venture capitalist that last year pumped £24m into the company in return for a 25% stake. Needless to say, the 'another magazine' didn't really materialise beyond a one-off issue of a magazine called *Trash*. The industry—publishing especially—was contracting in front of our eyes. This was *The Guardian*'s analysis:

'Readers have also deserted the magazine, which was once the biggest selling title in the sector. In the last set of ABCs,

Ministry's circulation fell 22% on the previous quarter to just 65,030. Ministry of Sound creative director Mark Rodol said that the decision to close the magazine was not made for financial reasons, but because it had strayed too far from the image the company wanted to promote.'"

The bigger Gaunt Street-based brand had also spent a lot of money on more recent signings, and a pattern was starting to, well, "emerge." Back to the piece:

"Despite scoring early hits with acts such as So Solid Crew, recent signings such as US electroclash act Fischerspooner have proved less successful. Earlier this month, Ministry sacked its head of A&R, Matt Jagger. IPC, meanwhile, continued to work hard on *Muzik* magazine, despite sales figures dropping."

Back to Frank on the frontline, who correctly describes *Mixmag* and *Muzik* as "two different beasts."

"*Mixmag* had to be all things to everyone. Things like 'five-star clubbing' and the photos of people having a great time in clubs were really important, and a lot of that was driven by the adverts. The ad director, Pete Fox, who had worked at IPC, was a visionary. He set out to make clubs the focal point of the advertising, and it became really competitive to see which club would take out the biggest spread or back cover. Those ad pages were the backbone of the magazine. The ad team was way more rock 'n' roll than the journalists and was closest to the club promoters: it was the symbiotic art of the jigsaw puzzle."

"When *Mixmag* was being bought by EMAP, Tony and Christine sold up. Fair play, I say—they were due a payday for dedicating their entire lives to dance music and DJ culture. *Muzik* then got in touch: Ben was taking a job at Deconstruction and doing a couple of days a week at each. Push was still the editor, and when Push left, Ben came back full-time."

"I went to *Muzik*, and it was quite a different culture. *Muzik* was owned by IPC, so in a lot of ways, it was a lot more professional than *Mixmag*. There were things like actual sub-editors, whereas at *Mixmag*, the assistant editor did all the subbing. There was a production editor to make it run smoothly, because it was owned by people who ran magazines for a living. At its very core, it was a company that knew how to make magazines. The primary difference in culture would be that at *Mixmag*, it was journalists who had trained in English or as journalists. Alexis Petridis was a Cambridge English graduate. These people took the writing and journalism very seriously. And you can see that, because all those people went on to succeed in journalism rather than dance music. Dom Philips with his political and ecological writing in Brazil, Andy at *Q*, Alexis at *The Guardian*. At *Muzik*, the team was far more embedded in dance culture, and the journalism was perhaps slightly secondary."

But the magazine was starting to fragment. It was one part *Death in Vegas*, two parts *Groove Armada*, and three parts *Cream* and *Gatecrasher*. Looking back, I can see that I used my time there to hone my skills, learn as much about house, techno, and hip hop as possible (I would always consider weekends with *Vibe Magazine* as "hip hop homework") and watch how the battle lines were being drawn with the suits upstairs in the IPC Tower, which, thankfully, felt further away than when we later returned there in 2002. But the key word is "learn."

"I had to put a different hat on and be a bit less about the music and more about how do we make this interesting to sell more copies," says Frank. "And the irony being, IPC, as a professional operation, meant I could buy records and expense them. There were loads of perks and positive sides. And it was a good culture. There was a fun post-work pub culture, getting to hang out with people from *Loaded*, *Melody Maker*, and *Uncut*. It was such an incredibly fertile time—an explosion of music, fashion, and dance music culture happening nationwide and internationally. So much so that there was easily room for more than one magazine."

There was, of course, one other culture beyond the walls of Hatfield House, and it was the culture of the DJ community itself. "Community" is a word that's used an awful lot these days to describe areas of club culture; another word that's bubbled to the surface is "spaces," and the third word that you hear relentlessly to describe a career path is "journey." In 1999, there was only one word that covered all of these (special) branches, and it was "the scene." Over to Frank: "There was a great team at *Mixmag* and a great team at *Muzik*, and I'd like to say that these magazines succeeded because we were geniuses, but the truth is dance culture was expanding exponentially throughout the '90s, and that created an audience hungry for information. We were a bunch of relative kids embedded in this culture that the older generation wanted a piece of but didn't really understand. So the grown-ups gave us all these toys to play with, make our mistakes, and learn from them. We were all lucky enough to be in the right place at the right time and got our feet in the door."

We'll leave Frank with one more thought before the story continues. "If you want my personal thoughts, Ben had a really strong vision for the magazine, but the problem with a major publisher is the publisher above the editorial team. And they were businessmen who just wanted to be bigger than *Mixmag*. One of the problems of capitalism: [I would say] why can't we be number two, but the Number One for underground music? The people above the editor would say, 'How do we kill the opposition?' So they constantly put everyone under pressure to become more like *Mixmag*. Before I left, we did an issue that didn't have a cover star. We had a really good end-of-1998 CD, and we had a picture of a pretty girl dancing on the cover. I'm not saying it's the most intellectual cover, but it remains the best-selling issue of *Muzik* of all time. Perhaps the more casual free CD audience were happy with a pretty girl rather than, say, LTJ Bukem."

Once Frank left, the original team we knew and loved had been heavily depleted. We still had our trusty Production Editor, Tom Mugridge, and his good friend, the caustic but undeniably brilliant Sub Editor, Duncan Bell, and the larger-than-life, Stetson-loving, Brighton-based writer, Thomas H Green, who did his best to steer the ship (literally sitting in Frank's hot seat). But while he was a most excellent mascot for a slightly counter-cultural life, he didn't have the confidence of the suits, and when a fourth (!) new editor was brought in, it was Thomas' time for the chopping block. I don't think he ever forgave the incoming music journalist Malik Meer for stepping over him for the main job, but for the first time since Frank departed, *Muzik* finally morphed into a credible, forward-facing music title. So the next year and a half under Malik felt to me like those early days of *XFM* must have felt to Stephen Merchant and Ricky Gervais: fun, life-affirming, edge-of-your-seat stuff where every day there was something new happening or a new idea being thrown into the ring for discussion and dissection.

I don't think that's how Thomas will remember it, but when there is a cast of characters this large and wide, not everyone will remember things the same way. Thomas' editorial stance was fairly and understandably anti-superclub, but they were still among our biggest advertisers, as Frank pointed out. In 2001, Carl Cox and Yousef had monthly columns, and the back page—now a quality Q&A called "Check Your Head"—made room for a variety of club and pop culture legends like soul crooner Errol Brown from Hot Chocolate, Phil Collins (of Phil Collins and Genesis fame), and Boy George (and I should know, as I did that last club-culture interview, obviously, and at this point, he needs no introduction).

But you could see that *Muzik*'s culture-shaping moment in the sun was starting to dissipate. Where else could Kosheen or The Avalanches get a print cover in 2001? The answer was pretty much anywhere, and as the industry started to contract in the UK for the first time, our ability to find the next superstar proved harder and harder. So instead, we would run covers with mid-tier artists, hoping that the interview itself would create some headlines. The Kosheen strapline tells you everything you need to know about the non-story: "From white label to white limo… in six weeks." Even the cover image lacked confidence.

There is one issue that I do still think very much stands up, and it was the Underworld cover from August 2002. The magazine was still edited by Conor McNicholas, but on the plus side, this particular issue was a hefty 146 pages (!) and the cover image, with Karl Hyde in the forefront, is still a classic shot two decades later. The straplines remain as limp as ever though: "The comeback album that will blow your mind!" It's not an album

CHAPTER EIGHT: TINY DANCER

that blew my mind too much back then, sadly. However, it did contain one of the top five best Underworld singles of all time, *Two Months Off*. The classic *Muzik* balance is there—all the main musical bases are covered, including the return of British trip-hop group Morcheeba.

Of course, we weren't just working in the office: I was out almost every night, and who wouldn't be when there was so much to take in? This was the era of Credence Records and *Days Go By* by Dirty Vegas, of Röyksopp [1] and their remix of Felix Da Housecat, and their sublime debut album *Melody AM* on Wall Of Sound. It was the era of the Audio Bullys, Tim Deluxe, Fatboy Slim on Brighton Beach, James Zabiela, Sasha's *Wavy Gravy* single and the accompanying, room-dividing album *Airdrawndagger*, and the glorious, ubiquitous *Lazy* by X-Press 2 and David Byrne—still an incredible pop/club moment for all parties involved. It was *Where Love Lives* retooled for Talking Heads-fixated house fans. We also gave them all a cover with David Byrne shot in New York, which unfortunately just looked like David had been photoshopped in (which he hadn't). But I don't want to take away from the song or from Skint Records in this era: X-Press 2 and Fatboy Slim, especially, took the Brighton label to the very top.

And even though Push remains fairly dismissive about some of those final covers, for me, every day was exciting again under the firm editorial direction of Malik. We'd been moved back to the main Kings Reach Tower and were now on the 25th floor, which, as someone who didn't like heights, was not ideal. But we

---

1 (Which translated into English means 'smoke mushroom')

had our plucky young publisher Richard Coles in the corner and a fresh new team that featured more women editorially (three!) than ever before. Magazine cover-wise, we made room for OutKast, James Murphy, Missy Elliott, and the Isle of Skye synth-pop sensation Mylo. These are not easy artists to get time with these days. We were still going on lots of trips—I still made it to Miami every year. However, there's no doubt that from issue 90 onwards, we felt that if Muzik was going to go down in flames, we would be shot down, to paraphrase mid-career Bon Jovi, in a blaze of glory.

But before this chapter comes to a close, I want to focus on one episode that, looking back, was something of a marker in the sand for me, not just editorially but also spiritually.

In 2001, I saw director Cameron Crowe's rock biopic *Almost Famous* for the first time, which is why I am calling this chapter *Tiny Dancer*.

A year later, I spent an incredible few days in America with the Brighton-based breakbeat DJ and producer Adam Freeland, who had been a *Muzik* favourite thanks to his cutting-edge breaks label Marine Parade. One of the best trips I ever went on; it took in Tampa and Miami with Adam, who not only named his label after the area he lived in by the beach but also had friends in the right places. He'd just made a record with my epic house buddy Brian Transeau called *Hip Hop Phenomenon* that I still hammer at home to this day, and he'd decided that America was there for the taking.

And while it was far from my best writing, this print feature definitely captured what it was like to be on the road (and on a tour bus!) with a young DJ in the ascendancy and hard ticket headliners, LA-born big-beat catalysts The Crystal Method. 28 at the time, Adam's music was genuinely pushing things forward and exploring experimental nu-skool corners that Sasha was equally excited by around the same time. And the song that was constantly played on the tour bus was *Tiny Dancer*. Let's cut to the end of the feature.

"Breakbeat's problem has been that there aren't enough DJs supporting it," says Adam. "There's only a handful with an international profile, whereas in drum n bass and prog, there's loads. I'm on a fucking mission! Honestly, there's so much incredible music out there!"

Suddenly, a lone Cadillac screeches from out of nowhere.

"Hey Adam!" hollers the driver. It's a fan from the gig. "Wanna come to a party?"

Almost Famous? Not bloody likely.

Andy Crysell's Sasha cover feature outro had made its mark (the lesson of this chapter might be 'always steal from the best!') and while I can't pretend that my feature ending was as magical as Andy's, it was the best that I could do to sum up this brilliant Breakbeat Era.

But there was a much bigger issue brewing beyond the one I was working on.

I landed back to the most messages I'd ever experienced before buying a Blackberry and experiencing BBM. It was September 11th, 2001.

CHAPTER NINE
WHEN THE MUZIK ENDS

There are three issues from *Muzik*'s final print run that I revisit frequently for research and nostalgia, and there's a compelling reason for that: during the mid to late nineties (referring to issue numbers rather than decades), the colourful covers truly stood out. Equally memorable were the attached covermount CD mixes I curated, each meeting my own high internal quality standards. These included contributions from MJ Cole, Gilles Peterson, Cassius, and Erol Alkan, among others. They remain timeless, partly because we finally broke free from the constraints of progressive house (thanks to Malik's vision) and focused on music across a broad genre spectrum. We prioritised risk-taking over sticking to the familiar, championing experimental and diverse music rather than the predictable male-dominated, often homogeneous lineups booked in Kings Cross and Farringdon week after week. During this period, the *Diwali* rhythm captivated us all—credit Sean Paul, Wayne Wonder, and Lumidee for that, as well as the *Diwali Riddim Mix* on Greensleeves.

Issue 95: 'Disco Punk Explosion'. This issue came with an accompanying mix by Tim Sweeney, who is now a globally respected DJ and broadcaster running *Beats in Space* through its new home on Apple Music. The tagline on the CD screamed, "Revolution! Action! Now!"—but the music did all the talking. It featured tracks from Le Tigre, Playgroup, Metro Area, and the up-and-coming disco/punk/pop outfit The Rapture. To this day, I play this mix annually to remind myself of the richness of the genre, and The Rapture's big single, *House of Jealous Lovers*, remains a dancefloor destroyer.

Issue 98: 'Let's Get Ill!'. In this issue, *Muzik* secured a world-exclusive interview with the now-incarcerated P. Diddy, which infuriated *Mixmag*—they were the bigger title, but we were undoubtedly cooler. English writer Johnny Davis (a former editor of *The Face*) got the inside scoop on Diddy's empire and his plans to move into a new house. The accompanying CD featured a mix by a young, UK-based, Turkish-born rising star named Erol Alkan. His stellar mix included tracks from Playgroup, Goldfrapp, Headman, and a remix of The Faint by Jacques Lu Cont. While the process required considerable patience (Erol needed a lot of hand-holding), the result was undeniably worth it. Recently relicensed for Apple Music, this remastered mix remains a classic, epitomising the curation and artistry we aimed for. With CD players fast becoming relics of the past, streaming is now the best way to experience it. If pressed, I might argue that this was the finest mix ever attached to the cover across *Muzik*'s 99 issues. [1]

And finally, we reach the fateful last issue of *Muzik*, featuring Outkast's Big Boi and Andre 3000 on the cover. We were midway through producing issue 100—so close to the milestone!—when

---

1 (And yes, I am aware this is subjective!)

we were abruptly shut down in a surprise meeting by IPC. Even now, 20 years later, I marvel at those photos of our Atlantean hip-hop heroes.

A quick summary of issue 99: *The Hot 50* featured the return of Outkast (another world exclusive), with additional pieces on LCD Soundsystem (we were big fans of James Murphy and his crew), Dizzee Rascal, Radio Slave, Richard X, and Ewan Pearson. The accompanying cover mix came from French touch masters Cassius and ranks as one of the strongest mixes we ever featured. I managed to secure tracks from Daft Punk (!!), Black Strobe, and The Streets. The mix was recorded in a single take during a whirlwind trip to Paris, where I had to catch the Eurostar to meet Cassius' manager, Pedro Winter—but more on that later.

The back page perfectly captured the magic of the era: a lineup split between *(We Love) Sundays At Space*, featuring Steve Lawler, James Zabiela, and François K; and *Rooty*—the legendary night run by Felix B (Basement Jaxx), Frank Tope, and Tayo. Plus, *Carl Cox and Friends* took over Tuesdays at Space for eight nights only, in collaboration with Angels of Love. What a time to be alive!

Credit must go to Malik for his innate desire to rip up the rulebook. In 2002 and 2003, BBC Radio 1 was still a major tastemaker, but perhaps the only DJ with a similarly eclectic vision to *Muzik*'s "anything goes" ethos was Mary Anne Hobbs with her *Breezeblock* mixes, which seamlessly blended mainstream and underground. Like one of our final cover stars, The Streets, we were all about pushing things forward wherever possible.

These three issues not only captured the spirit of summer 2003 but also showcased artists I still support today, particularly Outkast and LCD Soundsystem. By this point, the magazine cost

£3.80—a far cry from its launch price of 95 pence in '95. However, with cover mixes so central to the magazine's appeal (and sales), it's not surprising that *Mixmag* started trying to poach me. They were putting out CDs with names like *Nic Fanciulli – Porn House* (cue shudders).

Since that iconic Paul Oakenfold *HOME* issue, *Muzik* had occasionally ventured into mainstream territory (the *Groove Armada* CD with *The Chemical Brothers* on the relaunched cover was probably Conor's peak). Yet just before Conor joined, we landed Eminem (!) for our 5th birthday cover, accompanied by a brilliant Carl Cox mix CD that sold 40,000 copies—the highest sales during my full-time tenure. Under Malik's leadership, we gained fresh talent, including Features Editor Victoria Goodwin, Picture Editor Kate Dwyer, Message Editor Lauren Cochrane, and Clubs Editor Simone Baird (an early champion of Erol Alkan in the Kings Reach office). I also want to shout out Art Editor Declan Fahy, who was with me throughout my tenure and produced fantastic work. Declan was assisted by Dan Delaney, a super-nice young designer with a passionate love for music. (Dan's predecessor, Nick, was a slightly grumpy deep house enthusiast who didn't always appreciate direction.)

By this point, we wanted to be a cool, creative team and even added playful touches to the editorial process. For example, on the contents page, we'd pose a fun question, much like *Empire Magazine* did. One such question was: "Our favourite disco punk tracks are…"

- **Malik Meer**: ESG – *Moody*
- **Duncan Bell**: Big Black – *Kerosene*

- **Declan Fahy**: Howlin' Wolf – *Smokestack Lightnin'*
- **Dan Delaney**: The Numbers – *Intercom*
- **Ralph Moore**: The Cure – *Just Like Heaven*
- **Kate Dwyer**: The Dead C – *White Horse*

That cover mix from Tim should soon be making its way to Apple Music, as he and I have been discussing it throughout the year while I work on this book.

There's no doubt that electroclash and disco punk, as we called it, defined the sound of the moment in London and New York. The mix itself is a brilliant, brilliant time capsule of that era. "We thought this would be a good way to start off the mix," Tim said about *Orange Area* by Metro Area (who would soon sign to Virgin Records), in the magazine. "Metro Area is a tough cookie to remix, but I think we came through with this interpretation: live disco drums, live disco bass, and a big 10CC moment. Lovely."

I highly recommend this mix to anyone who loves classic DFA, early LCD Soundsystem, or who missed the heady days described in the book *Meet Me in the Bathroom*. [2] *Beat Connection* also features, remixed by James Murphy himself. "If I didn't put it in the mix, he would have beaten me or cried," said Tim with a wink. "I'm not sure which is worse." The mix concludes with a track by The Juan MacLean, which Tim describes as "angry robot funk."

Aside from Erol's mix and Miss Kittin's era-defining *Electroclash* mix a few months earlier, I don't think our cover mixes ever got better than this one in terms of quality. I remember Malik

---

2 By Lizzy Goodman, a fantastic read and now a TV documentary too.

and I working to clear tracks right up until the last minute, but we pulled it off. The mix itself was sent via courier from New York, and we managed to master it with just one day to spare. Dance music deadlines in 2002 were always like this: no one ever finished early, and no project was without its share of drama.

Issue 98 is definitely contentious through the lens of 2024, as it features former Bad Boy and P.T. Barnum alumnus, P. Diddy. He had discovered dance music through early trips to the Balearics and connections with figures like former Soul II Soul producer Nellee Hooper. Coming from hip-hop, Puffy was seemingly an early advocate for electro and techno, thanks to his friendships not only with Nellee but also with Felix Da Housecat, with whom he created the track *Jack U*. For this cover, however, he was here to discuss *Let's Get Ill*, a record featuring a variety of star collaborators: Kelis on vocals, with Deep Dish on remix duty. Puff, Nellee Hooper, and Kelis are all credited as producers, and while the track didn't set charts ablaze on either side of the Atlantic, it did kick off Puffy's annual pilgrimages to Ibiza. Around 2004 and 2005, he became a familiar sight at DC10 with his whistle or at Pacha, often accompanied by a fan (or several).

He would go on to collaborate with DJ Hell, Richard X, Erick Morillo, and Deep Dish in various guises. His DJ Hell collaboration, *The DJ*, was released on International DJ Gigolo, complete with a Radio Slave remix. At the time, it felt like Puff Daddy was infiltrating several corners of the club scene. Writing this now, as increasingly serious allegations emerge about him, I can't help but wonder what was happening behind the scenes. Yet back then, this crossover of such a global superstar into the world of dance music felt undeniably intriguing.

CHAPTER NINE: WHEN THE MUSIK ENDS

Johnny Davis did an excellent job with the interview, despite a very short window of time. Judging by the article's length and the inclusion of quotes from Deep Dish, Felix Da Housecat, Richard X, and Nellee Hooper, it couldn't have lasted more than 20 minutes. The only artist from this era of Ibiza who came close to matching Diddy's level of star power on the white isle was Madonna, who was also known to frequent DC10 during her visits to the island.

But we move on. Issue 98 also featured a deep dive into Brazilian drum 'n' bass, an interview with Daft Punk by Kevin Braddock (Thomas Bangalter quips, "The music industry is getting worse!" in a piece hilariously confined to two pages), a *One Louder* feature on Erol Alkan (and his cat) by new staff member Vic Goodwin, and a story on the Diwali rhythm by Alex Rayner. And then we arrived at Issue 99. Everyone needs a '99 once in a while.

The *Hot 50* issue reminds me a lot of the Paul Oakenfold cover from earlier years. Whatever you think of the cover itself, it's important to note IPC's historically rigid attitude toward featuring Black artists. Titles like *NME* and *Melody Maker* tended to favour acts like The Stone Roses, Nirvana, and The Beastie Boys over artists of colour. However, *Muzik* did its best to approach these matters with inclusivity. Unlike, say, *Ministry*, we cared deeply about our community and its people.

Over the years, larger-than-life figures like Carl Cox have remained hugely popular cover choices—and he's still one of the world's biggest DJs three decades later. But we also gave the spotlight to icons like Roni Size, Fabio and Grooverider, Bukem, and Goldie. On the house, garage, and techno front, we featured legends such as Kevin Saunderson, Wookie, and Kelis.

One standout was the iconic April 2000 shoot with Kelis, which was paired with the now-famous sell line, "We love you so much right now—AARGH!" I can still picture that vibrant green cover!

The *Hot 50* issue encapsulated my worldview in the summer of 2003. Common was featured[3], and Bob Sinclar Did Us A Tape. Whatever your later thoughts on dance-pop Sinclar, his cassette was formidable. When he wasn't crafting mainstream-friendly hits, he was delving into gems like Soft Cell, Martine Girault, and Frankie Knuckles' peerless *Whistle Song*. At heart, Bob's taste in disco was as impeccable as Frank Tope's had been in the 1998 *Muzik* office, which is why it deserves a mention.

His tape only improves as it progresses, with side two featuring Malcolm McLaren, X-Press 2, and Neneh Cherry's *Buddy X*. Bob clearly knows his onions, which makes it all the more shocking to recall his later suggestion that the world should—well—ahem—"Hold On."

"When I was 16, I used to go to this really small club in Paris," Bob recalled of his early eighties Soft Cell memories in the piece. "They played all this new wave kind of stuff. *Tainted Love* is a fantastic song that still sounds up-to-date—and futuristic."

He's absolutely right, of course—and his assessment of *Tainted Love* holds true twenty years later!

Elsewhere in the issue, I interviewed Richard X, and Kevin Martin reviewed Dizzee Rascal's debut album. Before he later evolved into The Bug, Martin remarked, "This record reduces the congested dance market to virtual redundancy." There's also

---

3 (*Electric Circus* was the fifth and arguably the bravest studio album by the still-rising American rapper)

a very early quarter-page advert for Rune's *Calabria* on Credence—a sign of the track's future ubiquity. [4]

With hip-hop so prevalent, we just wanted to keep being a cool, creative team. So, once again, we posed a question to the editorial team on the contents page:

"Our fave new things in dance are…"

- **Malik Meer**: Common/Stereolab/Playgroup (Malik Meer had impeccable taste)
- **Declan Fahy**: Tiga's *Hot In Herre* video
- **Daniel Delaney**: The Numbers
- **Ralph Moore**: "Afro-flavoured French house"
- **Carl Stroud**: Master H
- **Emma Robertson**: *Crazy In Love*

Yes, the era of Beyoncé was upon us.

As for the cover mix from Cassius's Monsieur Zdar, it was so delayed—despite my daily phone calls—that I uncharacteristically lost patience. By the third week of the four-week deadline, I told Cassius's manager, Pedro Winter, that I'd be taking the Eurostar to Paris to pick it up in person. (This was the only time in my career I've felt the need to take such decisive action!)

I'd had no direct contact with Zdar or Boombass—a situation that, in my experience, was never a good sign. Pedro kept assuring me, "It will be done," but after ten days of no progress and

---

[4] (Rune, for those slightly new to this game, is Rune Reilly Kolsch, and this was the beginning rather than the 'Destination Unknown'.)

with the final mastering deadline looming just five days away, I decided enough was enough. The next day, I arrived at Pedro's now-infamous Ed Banger office to find him calm and collected, the long-awaited CD sitting serenely on his desk. While Pedro appeared unruffled by my unannounced arrival, it had apparently been a different story earlier that morning when he'd banged on Zdar's door at dawn. "The man from *Muzik* is coming!" he had warned Philippe, who, in a panic, grabbed a handful of records and CD-Rs. "You must do the mix now!"

The mix, despite the chaos, was surprisingly excellent, with only a couple of wonky transitions. It captured the French electro scene effectively, and we even featured the Cassius logo on the cover of the CD—something that made my 28-year-old self immensely proud. I still regret not keeping Philippe's original email describing the last-minute scramble. He'd written something like, "Bad mixing is the new good mixing," as part of his apology for the occasional shoddy transitions. Regardless, this was the only time I ever had to board the Eurostar to galvanise our European counterparts into action—and the mix was worth it. There's even a full page in the magazine dedicated to it.

Thankfully, part of Philippe's email was printed on the CD page in the final issue for posterity:

"I'm currently mixing an album for a French artist called Sébastien Tellier," it begins. "We finish at 4 every morning. I was supposed to do a mix for *Muzik* magazine, but again, I forgot the deadline. All I can remember is Pedro Winter banging on my door at 10 in the morning with a CD-R and a bunch of French Touch records under his arm. He explained it's now or never!"

("Love this!" said Pedro Winter when I reminded him of this moment during the summer of '24, as I was writing this chapter. At the very least, it makes for a great story.)

Black Strobe, Agoria and Daft Punk all feature but interestingly, the song Philippe Zdar calls "the best song of the year" on the mix is by Bergheim 34 on Klang. The name of the song?

"Random Access Memory."

CHAPTER TEN
MOVING TO A NEW MANOR

The end was nigh—but somehow, it was still incredibly hard to process.

As a team, *Muzik* had recently traveled to Milton Keynes to see Eminem perform live. Over two days, he was supported by D12, 50 Cent, and Cypress Hill. Back in '03, tickets were a mere sliver of what they cost now—even through resale platforms like Twickets. All three nights were just £30 a pop. We made our way to Milton Keynes Bowl by coach, a group that included Malik Meer, Vic Goodwin, our trusty designer Dan Delaney, and my good friend Helen McGuire. Helen, now a kick-ass business woman with a book of her own, was in '03 navigating club culture through a few weeks of work experience at *Muzik* before heading to Radio 1. *Muzik* had always been a great springboard. The four-hour hip-hop show was incredible—but it was to be our last office outing.

When *Muzik* shut its doors[1], we were all in shock for quite some time. It felt a bit like being told your secondary school

---

1 (Coincidentally, the same day that the legendary Hollywood actress Kathryn Hepburn died)

and everything in it had burned down. You felt terrible. Suddenly, there was no desk, no daily duties, and no feature planning ahead. The long weekends, once filled with work, were now unexpectedly your own.

Norman Cook very kindly offered me a place to stay and decompress. My identity as a writer—and maybe even as a person—was so deeply tied to the magazine that I suddenly realised my skills would need to find a new home.

We had all been working studiously on issue 100, but when we asked the suits if we could finish it, they refused, citing something they called "emotional publishing." I've always thought that was an odd turn of phrase, but I suspect it meant the decision was driven purely by numbers, not sentiment. Issue 100 would have been monumental (I was working on a cover mix featuring 50 tracks), but after the classic Outkast cover, I doubt the next issue's more generic image would have been as iconic—we didn't have Eminem or André 3000 to give it that extra star power.

As it stands, we finished the run one issue short of a full century. For numerologists and cricket fans, this is the epitome of frustration. However, there's now talk of a special one-off issue in 2025 to finally complete the set. I'll be the first to share the news if it happens!

I vividly remember the Monday morning when we were called into a meeting room. Something about the atmosphere felt off, and now we knew why: there would be no more *Muzik* that day—or ever again—on the 25th floor. The boutique *Muzik* Awards we had been planning for October 2003 were also scrapped. The triumphant 2002 ceremony in Hammersmith, which featured Massive Attack, Robert Carlyle, Zoe Ball, and Fatboy Slim, would be the last.

CHAPTER TEN: MOVING TO A NEW MANOR

I'd worked incredibly hard on that final ceremony, and it felt like everyone of note in the industry had turned up. Beyond Carl Cox, CircoLoco, and the others I've mentioned, Virgin Records' dance promo supremo Caroline Prothero brought along a young French protégé, a Paris-based DJ named David Guetta. He snagged the very last seat at the very last table just before the event began. The evening feels like a blur because I had so much to oversee, but I do remember Balearic DJ Phil Mison providing a brilliant pre-ceremony soundtrack.

The post-ceremony DJ guests included Gilles Peterson and Carl Cox. My favourite memory of the night was when a guest told me the awards had "real soul." I was utterly depleted by the end of it. Though my title was Assistant Editor, I was effectively the Executive Producer of an industry awards show that genuinely mattered. It's the only one from that era people still speak about fondly. (*Dancestar Awards* in London, run later by Ben, never quite captured the same spirit.)

I had pulled in every favour imaginable for guests, presenters, promoters, and even the sponsor—a cheap energy drink called Shark, which still somehow exists. Shark only came through at the eleventh hour, thanks to IPC's hard-working marketing team, including PR Manager Nicola Woods and Events Manager Pauline Carroll. Without their efforts, the entire event would have been canceled. And now, there would be no more *Muzik*, at least not in its current form. I felt bereft.

What on earth was I going to do next?

A few months earlier, I'd been contacted by Pauline Haldane at *Mixmag*. She asked me to meet her and the then-Editor, Viv Craske, in Soho. Pauline struck me as the brains of the operation, while Viv was polite and convivial—if a little bland in his taste. Viv seemed particularly keen to know how I had managed to secure such incredible artists for *Muzik*'s cover mixes. (The answer, of course, was simple: my net worth was my network, and by then my network far outstripped anything *Mixmag* could hope to tap into.)

To be blunt, *Mixmag* in 2003 and 2004 was somewhere between *Nuts* and *Zoo* in terms of its target demographic. It was slightly better than *Ministry Magazine* had been in 2002, but not by much. While it cared more about music, its focus was largely mainstream. If you were into Goodgreef, Sundissential, or frugging (now there's a word I don't use anymore) to Lisa Lashes, Fergie, or BK, *Mixmag* was for you.

There were bona fide porn ads in the back of *Mixmag*, a *Porn House* CD on the cover, and a cover policy that had significantly deteriorated since Frank Tope's tenure in the mid-1990s. While *Muzik* embraced the entire dance spectrum and explored new, idealistic strands, *Mixmag* of this era leaned heavily into bikini-clad covers with headlines about drugs, cars, and sex. The magazine painted Ibiza as little more than a hotbed of hedonism, starting and ending on Bora Bora beach. In hindsight, I take back what I said about *Mixmag* in the mid-90s: compared to the brainless nonsense of my first few issues in 2003, it was a Picasso painting.

Wait—"my first few issues?"

At this point, my Plan A was to take a job at *Mixmag* to get onto the East London property ladder. My *Muzik* severance package included a significant tax-free payment, which allowed me to put a deposit on my first property in the now-gentrified E8 zone we call Hackney Central. The only other thing I needed was a steady job to secure a mortgage, so I joined

Mixmag almost immediately after *Muzik* closed. I had about three weeks off and listened to friends asking why I would buy a place in "Crackney."

BBC broadcaster Zoe Ball (now Mrs. Fatboy Slim) also texted me during this time, and I've never forgotten her sweet words: "Don't worry. One door closes, and another door opens."

She wasn't wrong. I initially thought the job would be a stopgap until the next adventure swept me back to the Balearics, but I ended up staying full-time until at least 2011. It's a very, very different beast now, I must add.

The only constants behind the scenes from 2004 are Nick Stevenson, who is as committed to the brand as anyone could be, and myself as a creative consultant. These days, I'm bringing in covers featuring the likes of James Blake, Gorillaz, Romy, Overmono, and Yaeji. My specialty remains spotting talent early and championing them long before the mainstream catches on.

But my first *Mixmag* issue? That was painful. So painful, in fact, that I don't even keep a copy in my archive. It featured the rotund American "comedian" Har Mar Superstar (remember him?) sitting in a hot tub. That's all I care to recall.

On the team was the intrepid Duncan Dick, and to my right sat Gavin Herlihy, a passionate and plucky Irish writer with a big heart and an even bigger love for techno, minimal or otherwise. We became fast friends and often made pilgrimages to DC10 on Mondays, joined by the magazine's techno editor, Ed Karney, who, like me, eventually transitioned into artist management. Thankfully, it was an era before smartphones, so our 24-hour Ibiza scrapes remain undocumented for modern audiences.

In my first months, I worked hard to make my mark on the music editorial. I brought in cover mixes like Jon Carter's (October 2003) and another project I'm still proud of, *New York Heroes*, compiled by none other than the now-vegan-dance-superstar Moby. I say "compiled" because it wasn't mixed—it was a proper compilation featuring tracks by Iggy Pop, Suicide, and Grandmaster Melle Mel & The Furious Five. Once again, I had worked my licensing magic.

Viv, however, began to show his editorial stripes.

"Why don't we call it a Moby DJ mix?" he suggested.

"Because he didn't mix it," I replied.

"Yes, but wouldn't that sound better?"

This was the start of friction within the team, as Gavin and I tried to balance our underground tastes with the broader, more mainstream clubbing editorial demands. Unfortunately, *Mixmag* was still catering to the *Nuts* and *Zoo* audience, which was massive in the UK at the time.

The publisher, Rimi Atwal, wasn't helping. When I secured an exclusive one-hour house mix from platinum-selling UK duo Groove Armada, she asked, "Why are we running a cover mix from a chill-out band?" Eye-rolling emojis didn't exist in 2005, but if they had, I'd have sent one her way. It was clear that even our publisher lacked genuine passion or understanding of the product.

This is precisely why I hadn't wanted to join *Mixmag* initially. I felt like I'd gone from the best editorial team to the most commercial. *Mixmag*'s owners, EMAP, also owned Kiss FM, which epitomized my concerns: no DJ I admired would have touched a Kiss FM show in 2004.

CHAPTER TEN: MOVING TO A NEW MANOR

Despite my misgivings, I dug into my Ibiza files to secure DJs who could elevate the magazine's credibility in 2004, 2005, and 2006. The roll call included Loco Dice, Steve Angello, Sebastian Ingrosso, Eric Prydz, Sven Väth, Carl Cox, and M.A.N.D.Y. One of my all-time favourite cover mixes from this era was by Armand Van Helden in 2005. Armand, now enjoying yet another renaissance (his sixth, perhaps?), delivered a stellar mix featuring his hits *Professional Widow*, *Spin Spin Sugar*, and *Hear My Name*. It rivaled any mix CD you could find at HMV on Oxford Street, and that was always the aim: a big name could sell an extra 5,000–10,000 magazines.

The *Mixmag* team wasn't as expert as the crack squad at *Muzik*, but we made it work. I also gained insight into how other print magazines operated. *Q Magazine* was filled with grumpy, highly opinionated middle-aged men with a declining product. Let's move on. *Mojo*, much older than *Q*, was infinitely nicer and wiser, which is why it's still very much thriving in print, complete with a cover CD. Then there was *Kerrang!*, which we'll come back to later.

Our second publisher, Nick Knowles, was a music man, and I liked him immediately. I delivered the mixes on time (just barely, as those pesky DJs always tested my deadlines), gradually improved *Mixmag*'s credibility, and worked alongside Gavin and Nick to maintain strong industry communication.

We still used a fax machine for licensing, working 10–6 in Soho, which meant evening activities nearby were easy to navigate. The End was still open, fabric was thriving, and cheeky electro hideouts like The Cross and The Key were buzzing. I was also making monthly trips to Ibiza, where I felt more at home than in Hackney. I knew Ibiza's roads better than the streets of Dalston or Stoke Newington.

By this point, Gavin and I were deeply immersed in the underground techno scene spanning London, Berlin, and Ibiza. Eventually, Gavin moved to Berlin to pursue his DJ dream, but I was content to stay in East London and frequent spots like The T Bar to catch Luciano or Ricardo Villalobos at boutique parties across the city. Secret Sundaze led the charge, alongside Mulletover, where my friends Rob Star and Stuart Geddes hosted regular 1,000-person parties. The music was dark and rich, though less melodic than the sounds I was used to hearing on the Space terrace. At *We Love* on Sundays, Paul Woolford, Miss Kittin, and James Zabiela kept things in a familiar lane, but by then, Mondays in Ibiza had become the domain of Cocoon on the Amnesia terrace.

Sven Väth reigned supreme, and this emerging sound gradually took over Ibiza's fringes before eventually dominating even its largest dancefloors. The vibe was edgy, electronic, and electrifying. Sven's trusted ally was Richie Hawtin, and together, they built a legacy that endures today through ventures like Timewarp. Other key players included Marco Carola, Luciano, Loco Dice, and Ricardo Villalobos, who initially stood firm with Cassy, the group's sole female resident DJ. (Cassy has plenty to say about this period, but it would require a chapter of its own.) Circo Loco, meanwhile, had its own queen in Tania Vulcano, the humble yet immensely talented DJ from Uruguay. She eventually recorded a seminal *Mixmag* CD for me—a Circo Loco mix featuring Martin Buttrich's *Full Clip*, arguably the most iconic track of that era, released on Carl Craig's Planet E imprint in Detroit.

As happens in any tight-knit scene, friendships fractured, and Sven watched his "techno Avengers" splinter as individuals pursued separate paths—often influenced by money. Despite this,

Cocoon remains my favourite Ibiza party of all time, and my editorial in *Mixmag* reflected its significance.

Looking back, it's hard not to see this period as a golden age for the underground techno scene, particularly in Ibiza. The music drove the culture, and while minimalism defined the sound and style, the experiences were unparalleled—intense, immersive, and unforgettable. In East London, the scene thrived with its distinctive mix of wonky haircuts and the biannual appearances of Richie Hawtin and his protégé, Magda. Our in-house "Animal" (from *The Muppets*), house editor Craig Torrance, championed Magda fervently.

However, we couldn't figure out how to stop declining sales.

In a pivotal move, EMAP, the company behind *Mixmag*, *Q*, and Kiss FM, decided to sell *Mixmag*. The buyer, Development Hell (now the magazine's long-time owner), also published *The Word*. Led by Jerry Perkins, Development Hell promised to revive *Mixmag* after years of decline following the downturn in dance music's popularity. While magazines like *Ministry* and *Muzik* had closed by 2003, *Mixmag* was still selling 46,470 copies per month. But it was clear: without a buyer, *Mixmag* might have been axed. I remain grateful to Development Hell for giving the title a new lease on life, even as legendary titles like *Smash Hits* faded away.

In the summer of 2005, *Press Gazette* reported the news:

> *"Development Hell, the publishing company behind The Word magazine, has promised to nurse struggling dance music magazine Mixmag back to health after buying it from EMAP. Publisher Jerry Perkins, who reportedly masterminded the*

> *purchase, said the company's focus on 'brands, not magazines' would be the tonic needed to get the title back on its feet after years of decline following the fall-off in interest in dance music. Rival titles Ministry and Muzik closed in 2000 and 2003, while sales of Mixmag fell at the last ABCs by 8 percent year-on-year, to 46,470."*

Following the sale, we relocated from central London to N1. For me, the change was minor—my focus remained on Ibiza, where I attended Cocoon after-parties filled with boats, beaches, and bottomless bubbles. Mischief was plentiful, and dancing and conversation blurred into 48-hour odysseys. Sven was the undisputed leader of this glamorous chaos, accompanied by a vibrant cast of characters, including dancers who later embraced wellness and DJs who found themselves replaced as the scene evolved, especially post-2020. Notable figures from this era include Maurizio Schmitz, Johannes Goller, Sarah Qaiser, Ida Engberg, Maya Boyd, Dubfire, Behrouz, Luciano, and even James Blunt, who turned out to be unexpectedly entertaining.

This era was magical—a beautiful time that still inspires me. The minute I landed in Ibiza, London faded away entirely.

Back in London, the move to King's Cross brought personnel changes. Pauline Haldane departed amicably, and Jerry Perkins brought back Andrew Harrison, a former *Mixmag* editor, to steady the ship. A sharp and detail-oriented editor, Andrew prioritised quality writing and features, ushering in stories on acts like Goldfrapp, Scissor Sisters, and—for one month only—Sam Sparro of *Black and Gold* fame. He also eliminated the gratuitous stories about cocaine and ketamine, reestablishing editorial integrity. With a proper editor at the helm, we got our groove and spine back.

By 2008, Nick Stevenson's role had shifted significantly. Fast forward to 2024, and he now serves as Managing Director of *Mixmag*, *Kerrang*, and *The Face*. But in those days, we were in the thick of an electro revival. Acts like Scissor Sisters, who had started as underground electro performers, were now signed to major labels like Polydor.

The CDs I curated during this era were strong—featuring Felix Da Housecat, Steve Angello, Carl Cox, Loco Dice, and Timo Maas. However, some cover decisions baffled even the artists' teams, such as when we featured the rock band Hard-Fi. Thankfully, the accompanying CD, mixed by Switch (of Major Lazer fame), included groundbreaking tracks for Hot Chip and others, cementing it as a standout mix.

By this point, I'd been in full-time magazine work since 1999 and felt it might be time for a new challenge outside journalism. Andrew Harrison departed to edit *Q Magazine*, replaced by the dynamic Nick De Cosemo. While his arrival brought energy, the product lacked the authoritative voice that had defined *Muzik*. Seeing so many disillusioned writers at *Q*, I vowed to avoid the same fate.

The writing was on the wall for print media, and if I couldn't stay ahead of trends, who could?

A couple of years later, a chance encounter at—where else?—fabric set me on a new path.

CHAPTER ELEVEN
THE CAN I GET ERA

I was at fabric late one Saturday night when I first heard *Coma Cat* by Tensnake—a record so huge and richly melodic that it dominated Ibiza for two straight seasons and eventually sold nearly a quarter of a million copies. That's actual, bona fide sales—not streams (which are now, of course, in the millions). The year was 2010, and CDs were starting to fade, though their decline wasn't yet as drastic as it is today. Back then, Mixmag was still selling 20,000–30,000 copies a month, but the once-coveted jewel case CD—formerly a major selling point—was losing its relevance. With CD players being gradually replaced by Sonos speakers and free SoundCloud accounts, and a little online portal called YouTube gaining traction, the justification for the cost of those CDs was diminishing.

It was a time before Boiler Room and Mixmag Lab, yet the major stars of today were beginning to emerge through festival bookings and crossover singles on the right labels. We're talking about Jamie Jones and Paradise, The Martinez Brothers, Loco Dice, and Marco Carola. Meanwhile, Scottish producer Calvin Harris was evolving from his electro beginnings—reminiscent of Mylo's *Drop the Pressure*—into one of the biggest pop-dance stars on the planet. His transformation (both musically and physically) was nothing short of spectacular, rivaling even Kim Kardashian's glow-up.

Dance music was becoming big business—especially for those in front of the curtain, rather than reporting from the sidelines. Clubs and festivals were the heart of the action.

Music-wise, it was the era of *Reckless With Your Love* by Azari & III, early Jessie Ware (*Devotion*, her 2012 debut, is still on repeat in my house), Bicep and their pre-stardom blog-house sound, and the incredible Disclosure remix of Jessie Ware's *Running*. (Credit where it's due: Mixmag nailed the timing with a brilliant Disclosure cover during this period. Their branding was equally spot-on.)

An opportune disco encounter with Marco Niemerski (Tensnake) changed the next ten years of my life.

The beautiful thing about fabric—then and now—is its ability to surprise. That Saturday night, Marco performed live, and the power of his record, with its unforgettable melody, compelled me to track him down. I was captivated not only by the musicality of *Coma Cat* but also by its sly vocal hook: *"Can I get, can I get, get."* I emailed Marco the Monday after the gig. He responded immediately: "I don't have a manager, and I need to think about publishing. I don't really know what to do with this single, but it's coming out soon on Permanent Vacation! I should probably think about these things."

This candid "thinking out loud" email sparked a new chapter. My first UK management partner, Oli Isaacs, and I saw the opportunity and flew to Germany to see Marco perform again, this time alongside his close friend, the scholarly DJ, producer, and remixer, Gerd Janson.

And that was it. With a handshake that weekend, we began managing Tensnake. Within months, we had a classy CD compilation with Defected titled *Tensnake In The House* (shoutout to A&R Andy Daniell for signing the project!) and an instrumental disco record added to Radio 1's C-List. In 2024, that record has gone silver—a remarkable achievement in an era where music sales have drastically declined. This silver certification is something I'm still very proud of, having helped bring it to the global market alongside Oli.

We followed up with *Mainline*, a cover of the Black Ivory '80s dance classic featuring UK singer Syron. Despite a solid black-and-white video and a great vibe, it didn't achieve the success we'd hoped for. Still, *Coma Cat*'s success marked the beginning of a new career in music for me—one where I collaborated with publishers, record labels, promoters, designers, pop stars, and engineers. This new role offered opportunities to explore and analyse the industry through features, podcasts, and later, radio (as I discovered during lockdown with Worldwide FM).

In many ways, I had been searching for something like this to sink my teeth into.

I had already co-founded a boutique dance label, Moore Music, with Oli Isaacs, who also managed This Is Music, a company with a carefully curated roster that included Simian Mobile Disco and Bicep. We released early music by London house and disco producer Midland (years before his *Final Credits* smash) and gained support from Sven Väth and Jamie Jones. However, I had never managed an artist before—it was an entirely new ballpark.

While co-managing Tensnake, I continued consulting for Mixmag, editing the Music Reviews pages and curating the monthly *Big Tunes* section. This included releases from Âme and Dixon, Mark Ronson, Paul Woolford, and Simian Mobile Disco, as well as German techno gems from Innervisions, Kompakt, and Carl Craig's remix of Tom Trago's *Use Me Again*.[1]

Uniting both the DC10 hordes and the glitzier dance floors across the UK and into Ibiza Town, the biggest Jamie Jones vocal record of this era was probably Azari & III's *Hungry For The Power*. It was indie enough for DC10 but still big-room enough for Pete Tong and Pacha. This track helped catapult Jamie—a former Ibiza worker and club kid—into the realm of superstar DJs. Signed to FFRR by Pete Tong, Jamie's signature tune with Hot Natured, *Benediction*, wasn't far behind. The track managed to unite almost everyone in the UK who had experienced sunshine and rave culture in 2011.

Mixmag celebrated the moment by putting Hot Natured—comprising Jamie Jones and his American rave partner, Lee Foss—on the cover of the print magazine. Around the same time, the duo played a sold-out live show at The Roundhouse, further cementing their status as key figures in the scene.

What a time to be alive! A new generation was beginning to embrace 4-to-the-floor beats.

Mixmag reflected this era, which was bigger, brasher, and unapologetically more focused on hooks and pop vocals. The Swedish House Mafia played a massive role in this shift.

Clubland was emerging from the minimal wave, particularly

---

[1] It's a decade on since these records first got marketed by Ministry of Sound as "Deep House", and as the Radio 1 DJ Jaguar recently commented, it might be time for some of these records to make a comeback.

in Ibiza, and the music was edging closer to the mainstream. Acts like Pharrell Williams were collaborating with the Swedes, while French dance star David Guetta was teaming up with some of the biggest pop stars on the planet. In many ways, Guetta recognised a window of opportunity and leapt through it. Speak to someone like Armand Van Helden, and he'll tell you that David is the reason dance music reached its current prominence in America.

Following his crossover pop hit *When Love Takes Over* (heavily indebted to Coldplay's *Clocks*), it seemed everyone in hip-hop and soul wanted a piece of the new production-pop trend. David's success shifted the industry inexorably toward the mainstream. His biggest hits were custom-built for radio, particularly American radio, setting a new standard for dance music's global appeal. [2]

The tables were turning harder than ever toward commerce. Suddenly, Coldplay was collaborating with Swedish EDM stars like Avicii, while David Guetta was making records with hip-hop artists like Kid Cudi, UK chart-toppers Little Mix, and even global teen megastar Justin Bieber. This shift demonstrated how far electronic pop had come since the days of Inner City, Soul II Soul, and Fatboy Slim dabbling with the inner and outer edges of indie-pop. David, in particular, knew no limitations (some might say no shame!) when it came to concocting hits for the masses. While only a handful of his tracks have truly stood the test of time, there's no denying his role in opening the floodgates

---

[2] (His manager, Caroline Prothero, was instrumental in all of this: at the very last Muzik Awards, she brought David and introduced him to everyone present as a relative newbie outside of France: so that evening he surely shook hands with Circo Loco, Carl Cox and Gilles Peterson alike.)

for EDM worldwide, helping transform dance music into a billion-dollar industry.

As EDM records and artists gained traction in the US, so did a homegrown festival culture, ranging from the gargantuan Electric Daisy Carnival in Vegas to more underground festivals across the States. For once, American artists weren't looking to the UK for validation—they were finally being celebrated at home. Some, like Steve Aoki, gravitated toward the glitz of Las Vegas club culture rather than the melodic, drum-heavy underground sounds Europe favoured. You could add superstar names like Tiësto, Afrojack, and, by 2024, UK producer and Ibiza Rocks DJ Joel Corry (a former *Geordie Shore* star), to this list. No longer fixated on underground credibility, they were more interested in global domination and brand-building. Or, as David Guetta once famously said, "I'm not interested in being credible. I want to be IN-credible!"

It was a good time to be a DJ, no matter your lane.

In 2011, after we'd signed *Coma Cat* to Defected for a global single deal, *Mixmag*'s editorial team independently voted it their single of the year (no need for me to bribe anyone with cake or a weekend trip to Germany!). The track remains a timeless recording, a feel-good anthem that brings a smile to my face every time I hear it. It's one of those songs, like Fatboy Slim's *Praise You* or Inner City's *Big Fun*, that lives in the ether. For an artist, having one of these tracks can be career-defining. Just look at Robbie Williams' *Angels*, Peggy Gou's *(It Goes Like) Nanana*, or David Guetta's *Titanium*. These songs become the reason people come to your shows, and that can only be a good thing.

The bigger the dance music scene became, the more it evolved from being a 'party' into a 'show,' where audiences expected to hear the hits they'd been playing at home. And then, of course, there's the pressure of delivering those hits live.

The biggest lesson from *Coma Cat* was that anyone with a love for quality disco—whether it was Annie Mac, Pete Tong, Resident Advisor, or Radio 1's daytime playlist—would take notice. I still hear it blaring from windows, revived on the radio, and it remains the biggest record I've ever worked on professionally. I'm proud to have been there from the very beginning.

The track put Tensnake on the map as a "nu-disco" producer (a term he hated!) but also allowed me to connect the dots and tell a behind-the-scenes story that journalism couldn't. Over the next five years, we signed Tensnake to Virgin Records for an album, put together an *Essential Mix* inspired by *Breaking Bad*, remixed London Grammar and Little Dragon, collaborated on two tracks with the soon-to-be-ubiquitous Nile Rodgers of Chic and one with Jacques Lu Cont and helped usher in British pop-soul singer MNEK, who later skyrocketed via Gorgon City. We even played a one-hour live show at Melt Festival in Germany.

There was no stopping that *Cat*. Originally released on January 25, 2010, and re-released on September 20, 2010, through Defected and Permanent Vacation, the song only reached number 85 in the UK Singles Chart. However, it made the C-list on Radio 1 and helped usher in a higher standard for dance music on the station's daytime playlist. In some ways, Tensnake walked so Todd Terje and Gorgon City could fly.

The track's ubiquity ensured we were never short of show offers. Tensnake, now in a relationship with my good friend and trusted company bookkeeper Yvette, began jetting around the world in search of the next party. Early on, I accompanied him to shows in

Toronto and New York—a non-stop whirlwind featuring a cast of characters as vivid as any movie. My role as manager quickly expanded to include tour support, therapist, creative sounding board, and even psychiatrist. Many of the collaborators we encountered—Stuart Price, Nile Rodgers, MNEK, and even the brilliant album artwork designer Leif Podhajsky, who later crafted the brilliant visual world for Tame Impala—joined our orbit through brainstorming sessions and chance encounters on tour.

I vividly remember an early dinner in Miami with Marco and Nile Rodgers. Watching Marco starstruck as Nile regaled us with stories at Joe's Stone Crab in Miami Beach was a moment I'll never forget.

Nile Rodgers is a sweetheart—someone I've interviewed countless times since then. He even featured in the video and on the print cover of *Mixmag* with Marco when *Glow* dropped via Virgin in 2014. But at that particular dinner, he was sharing stories about Studio 54, Duran Duran, and an upcoming single he had in the works with the returning French disco heroes, Daft Punk. Though he couldn't reveal much about it so early in the process, the anticipation was palpable. Nile was also a fan of *Coma Cat*, which felt like a seal of approval from one of the greats.

That evening remains one of the most unforgettable musical experiences of my life.[3]

Virgin Records went all in, funding a poster campaign around East London for the *Mixmag* cover and the lead single, *Love Sublime*. The track not only featured Nile and Fiora Cutler—his

---

3 and Nile was a genuine fan of 'Coma Cat', which is also a pretty beautiful thing to hear, all told.

future girlfriend and a remarkable singer—but also came with an incendiary club mix from Duke Dumont. Duke, of course, would later top the UK charts with *Need U (100%)*. At the time, it felt like the stars were aligning—or so we thought.

In my mind, *Glow* represented Tensnake exploring a slightly different lane than his earlier singles, like *Holding Back My Love*.

His releases on Running Back were disco perfection, but now he was redefining pop music by channeling his early-1980s influences. These included Chic, Jellybean Benitez, and the British pop quartet Prefab Sprout—whose influence is unmistakable throughout *Glow*. However, as a sensitive artist, he was deeply affected by some of the album's reviews, which, despite these missing the mark in many ways, upset him.

Here's an excerpt from Pitchfork's 5.7 review:

"It's been nearly four years since *Coma Cat*,' and Niemerski has remained reliable. So *Glow* seeks to both capitalise on that reputation and introduce him to a larger audience—it's not only his debut album but also his first release on a major label. Successful dance full-lengths generally take one of two approaches: a statement of purpose separate from the creator's established style, or a collection of existing singles rounded up as a primer for newcomers. *Glow* goes in a different direction, offering a streamlined, sanitised version of the Tensnake sound. It's house music in miniature form, heavily brushed with disco's steady-handed bounce and tempered with just enough potential pop-crossover appeal.

Much of the album finds Niemerski collaborating with Berlin vocalist Fiora, a capable singer whose understated qualities make her both malleable and forgettable. Save for *See Right Through*—a moody cut that's made the rounds over the past year—Fiora's presence feels more like a placeholder, a paperweight meant to anchor the barely sketched house figures. Many of *Glow*'s songs are just-there, but a few manage to be engaging: *No Relief*, *See Right Through*, and *No Colour* are perfect examples of Niemerski's still-considerable talent with house form. The latter two tunes made memorable appearances on his Essential Mix, confirming that he's most in his zone when dreaming of the dancefloor.

The appropriately slow *58 BPM* is a lush, swarming synth-pop tune that serves as the album's strongest vocal cut, while album bookends *First Song* and *Last Song* play around with pop-focused drone while embracing the type of epic beams found in M83's music (or *Random Access Memories* own jet-engine closer, *Horizon*)."

Meanwhile, *RA* went even further, thanks (!) to Andrew Ryce:

"Marco Niemerski's music is cheesy, but we love him for it. His knack for deliriously happy songs (*Coma Cat*, his remix of *Reckless With Your Love*) has led to brushes with the mainstream, which he finally embraced with 2012's *Mainline* on Defected, a rote exercise in '90s vocal house that only earned him a bigger audience. Now he's signed to Astralwerks, and with the full force of the pop machine behind him, *Glow* is his unmistakable grab at the charts—but one still suffused with some of that old Tensnake glimmer. The resulting album is every bit as conflicting as that sounds.

Glow dumbs down Niemerski's music into mass market-ready chunks. It's like he's taken a coat of plastic wrap and applied it liberally to the whole album, leaving it texturally uniform and smooth, but curiously distant. There are wrinkles in such an all-encompassing approach, particularly the instrumentals, which are so atrocious it's hard to fathom why they were included at all. Thankfully, the majority of *Glow* features vocalists to fill the blanks. Outside of two spots from Jeremy Glenn and Jamie Lidell, the album may as well be credited to Tensnake and Fiora, the Australian singer who steals the spotlight from her producer more than once. Fiora makes a fine foil. Her breathy ad-libs are hooks in themselves, she's emotive without overdoing it and she tackles generic pop fare with real enthusiasm. She's the kind of guest you might imagine on a Disclosure track—which is probably a better reference point for *Glow* than anything in Tensnake's discography. *Glow*'s most successful songs channel the demure sexiness of lite FM radio, bolstered with powerful basslines and floor-ready percussion. The bumping Nile Rodgers collaboration *Love Sublime*, the sultry *Kill The Time* and the yearning *No Relief* are all excellent fodder for a more mature pop playlist. To his credit, though, he generally avoids rehashing *Coma Cat*, only borrowing its vibe for the album's one decent instrumental, *Things Left To Say*.

So, harsh words, but then the clue is in the word 'critic.'

The record sold around 40,000 copies, and while that's impressive for a dance album, it was definitely slim pickings compared to what was happening over in the Daft Punk camp. In 2016, five years after our journey had begun, Tensnake decided it was time to change management. While it was personally a very sad moment for me, as I'd watched his career and star rise as an artist, I soon realised that I didn't miss the babysitting—and I also didn't have to manage his expectations anymore. If you want some final unvarnished truth, I would say that Marco and I both loved quality disco pop with a passion, and we achieved some amazing things together. It's better to step away before a career starts to falter, but let's not take away from the success stories: at his white-hot house music peak—the tropical instrumental *Congolal*, the timeless early Running Back releases, the Sven Väth at Amnesia-supported remix of *Holding Back My Love* by Tiger and Woods, and the incredible super-early Kaytranada remix of *Feel of Love*—these records are still as amazing as any I have championed in my twenty-five years behind the wheel. They're perennial all-timers, and that's truly amazing.

But if part of this book is to be a reflection of times past and present, it would make sense to speak to Sarah Crane, who, while now at Defected as Director of Marketing and Operations, worked tirelessly behind the scenes marketing *Glow* and all its assets while she was at Virgin.

"I still love that record," says Sarah, who resisted pressure from the label to make the album artwork feel more "Ibiza-flavoured." "Ten years ago, there was a much smaller media landscape. Radio, a few TV ops, print media, and some titles with more clout than others were all prevalent, whereas now you have all the social media channels. It's the same size audience, but to reach them, you need to do more things. Growing awareness happens in a different place."

So, a *Mixmag* print edition cover was a huge deal ten years ago because it was one of the main focal points of the entire campaign. Radio played its part, but both print and radio have less power across the board now. There are many top-tier artists who got print covers then—Boys Noize, Diplo, Nina Kraviz, Maya Jane Coles—who probably look back fondly at what you'd have to call a marker in the sand for them career-wise.

A *Mixmag* cover was a statement, and I was lucky enough to write a few of them, although the Tensnake cover, with Marco's suggestion, was written by the writer and acid house historian Bill Brewster, who did a great job telling the story.

"There are still moments where that can happen," she adds cheerfully. "But now those brands that were once about print are now working in a digital space. It's about finding authorities in music, whether that's *Mixmag*, an Instagram page, or an influencer. It's still the same logic—tastemakers sharing what's hot with their audience. It's the format that's changed. And it's much more fractured. Radio is still important, but it might also be something posted on Instagram and TikTok.

"It's about having moments in as many places as possible. There might be a song on Instagram, and then a DJ at a party plays that song, and it seeps into their world through those touchpoints. It's live, TV—which is no longer linear—and mostly digital channels. And making these things happen in a consolidated time space so a frequency is built up."

So, is it harder?

"It's harder. There's more you have to do. Once you did advertising around one weekend, and it was all targeted to an impact moment. Whereas now we have on-air, on-sale, so it's about building an artist's audience, and that's about growth. There are so many places to find an audience. There's a very fractured magazine and press landscape. Influencers or personalities are important, and TV pluggers are mostly gone. It doesn't create an impact anymore! I can't think of a moment in my current world where I would buy a print ad. It's a large amount of money, and it's not a one-week moment anymore. You're building over time and making your budget go the distance. You've often got nothing left! Digital content has a longer lifespan online, and things can have viral moments later."

"Even ten years ago, a really good Radio 1 play would make a difference. It's all now cumulative—the odd spot play doesn't really touch the sides. It's an evolving world. It's how we market and expose our music to people that matters."

Tensnake introduced me to a world of masters and publishing, major labels and indie mentality, remixes for cash and for swaps, videos with Nile Rodgers, promo opportunities in Miami, Ibiza, and Australia, trips to New York to visit old and new friends, and to stop off at the iconic Ghostbusters fire station at 55 Central Park West—and of a life less ordinary. I'm still of the same multitasking mindset today, mainly because this simply isn't a world where you can survive solely as a music critic—not anymore.

And that's really the lesson of this chapter: spinning several plates creates more hot dinners.

CHAPTER TWELVE
FREETOWN CHRISTIANIA

After five years of running around the world with Tensnake, it was time for a change. The pressure of delivering another hit in the vein of *Coma Cat* had never quite materialised, despite everyone's best efforts—and not even the might of Virgin Records could conjure one up. Caught between his original underground roots and the rampant commercialism demanded by a major label, he found himself stuck between two musical stools and wasn't sitting comfortably on either by 2016.

The same thing had happened to Hot Natured and countless other electronic acts trying to scale the mountain with major label marketing. Once you've made the leap to a major, it's very, very hard to go back to your roots and expect forgiveness from original fans, who often feel like you've left them behind. This has happened to many DJs who score hits and suddenly find themselves headlining festivals, playing to crowds of up to 10,000 adoring fans. You've made your pact, but don't expect tastemakers to follow you up Ben Nevis.

As for me, I was ready for a break from full-time management and was enjoying the other projects coming my way, including the occasional *Mixmag* cover feature. In 2017, I wrote two—this was the first. One thing to say about *Mixmag* in 2017: it was a genuinely credible, must-read magazine again. The right team had come together.

I think my Kölsch cover feature is the only piece I've written that comes close to capturing the romance and excitement Andy Crysell conjured with Sasha's *Muzik* magazine cover back in October 1999. The Kölsch[1] issue came out in 2017, although by that point, we had stopped producing the once-essential cover CDs. The mix was now available only via a SoundCloud link and accompanied by a digital interview—and that's precisely where things stand today.

There are quite a few reasons why Rune Reilly Kölsch, aka Kölsch, and I are friends. One would be that we share a very similar taste in music and aesthetics. Rune is signed to the influential Cologne-based dance label Kompakt, a label whose history and impact on the industry are impossible to ignore. The label is run by Michael Mayer, another DJ and producer with impeccable electronic taste, and Rune is one of their priority album artists. He's also renowned in the scene as one of the nicest people you could meet.

We're similar in age—Rune is 47—and over the years, he's worked with some of the best artists on the planet. Whether as a remixer or collaborator, his résumé includes names like London Grammar, Tiga, Michael Mayer, and Coldplay.

We're all lifers in this particular club. Rune and I originally met at Circo Loco during the very, very early days of the open-air

---

1 And the music nerds among you may already know that Sasha and Rune made a scintillating club record together: it's called *The Lights* and it's absolutely among the best things that either party have produced. to date: it sounds like something you'd have heard blasting from The Courtyard at Cream in the late nineties or early zeros.

CHAPTER TWELVE: FREETOWN CHRISTIANIA

club. It was a heady, hedonistic era, and we bonded there, as well as during all-night sessions at Pacha in Ibiza Town on Wednesdays or Fridays.

In May 2017, Kölsch's manager Henrik invited me to Copenhagen, Denmark, for a cover feature, and *Mixmag* was on board. So, off I went to the city for a couple of days with one main goal: to write a definitive artist feature. What follows is some of the original, longer, unedited copy, giving you a taste of Denmark and insight into what ultimately made Rune the musician he is today.

"A hippie commune founded in 1971 in the spirit of self-proclaimed autonomy, Christiania—sometimes known as Freetown—is a ten-minute drive from the center of Copenhagen, in the city's eastern part. Once you're parked by the river, you pass the first of several former army barracks, a dozen or more brightly painted lakeside homes, and, if you're lucky, a couple of graceful swans gliding beneath a bridge leading to the heart of this archaic but undeniably fascinating neighborhood. Once there, all bets—and cameras—are off, as the goods being sold on Pusher Street are not something residents want documented.

Don't expect to see people with flowers in their hair, either: in 2017, you could rent a bike, grab coffee at Månefiskeren, or buy fresh groceries at a cosy buffet called Grønsagen. Yet old habits clearly die hard in Christiania. We soon spot a wooden shed filled with children's clothing ready for donating or exchanging, depending on your mood. This is where our six-foot-four cover star lived with his family for the first few years of his life.

"Christiania is where I was born," says Rune as we drive to the commune early one Friday morning in April. "In the early '70s, a bunch of hippies decided to occupy an old military quarter.

My parents happened to be two of the first hippies to move in there, and it's basically been that way ever since. It's been part of Copenhagen and yet, equally, it hasn't. But it's been there for over 40 years now, so there's not a lot the authorities can do. Generations have lived there. It's based on this anarchic principle that everybody has to agree on something before they do it, which is an interesting way to run a society!"

It's a complex, fragile idea, as liable to exploitation as it is to freedom. "But there's something quite beautiful about the original idea of Christiania," Rune continues. "Over the years, they've expanded over old ruins or built things from scratch. At the same time, though, it's a place where the police seldom go because there's always big resistance to official authorities. For a long time, it spawned a lot of criminal activity in the form of drug sales. That was limited to weed and mushrooms, but still, selling weed in Denmark is illegal and punishable in the same way as selling harder drugs. That's why we can't take too many pictures—they're not very happy about that. Some don't care, but others don't want their picture taken. And then you have the old weird freaks who spiral into conspiracy theories the moment they see a camera…"

At age five, Rune's parents decided to leave the commune. "We moved out pretty quickly,' he recalls. 'At the time, in the 1970s, there was a resurgence of heroin addicts who decided they could do whatever the fuck they wanted. We moved to another collective further north in Denmark, and I'm very happy about that because a lot of my friends who stayed there as kids had really traumatic experiences with the "weed characters." Kids and junkies are not the best combination."

CHAPTER TWELVE: FREETOWN CHRISTIANIA

Christiania, however, has also given rise to some positive "hippy vibrations." Rune mentions Lukas Graham, the Danish pop band behind the massive hit *7 Years,* whose lead singer, Lukas Forchhammer, was also born in this 900-strong commune, albeit later. "A lot of creative people in Denmark were born there, from different generations. People I know in art, food, and music have strong ties to that place. It spawned a lot of interesting stuff."

Are you still in touch with any of them?

He nods. "I still meet people, and it's all good. But it's a strange place."

Born in 1977, which was also the name of his debut album on Kompakt, Rune is a reminder, like The Black Madonna last year, that life-affirming success doesn't necessarily have to happen in your early 20s – although he's is no stranger to hits under an alter ego or two (hands up how many of you knew that Rune was behind the seismic house smash 'Calabria' back in 2003?). But he caught the dance music bug back in his formative years in Copenhagen. Rune's parents divorced when he was still young, and he divided his time between the two of them. "There was a youth club where I started experimenting because I was skateboarding at the time and it's where I would go to feel free. I really appreciate the magic of that time: there would be breakdancers and a discotheque and a radio station, so I gravitated towards all that. I started DJing in 1989, 1990, trying to get attention from girls! I'd put on Technotronic and *Lambada* and that kind of crap. Then I started my first band, Rune And The Motherfuckers: I was the lead singer and we'd play early rap records and Prince covers… we were terrible!"

Rune's manager Henrik acknowledges the importance of Rune's all-conquering creative spark too, and he should know:

Olsen used to be one half of Danish chart-chomping dance duo Brother Brown. "First and foremost, he lives and breathes to unfold his creative musical ideas 24/7 whatever it takes, no compromises. He never goes for a safe and current sound solution, but always thinks about what he as an artist can bring for the future. It's very rare today." In the end, looking forward is the most important aspect. "Absolutely. That's the whole point of electronic music, to look forward. I like a retro record once in a while but it's extremely important that we push the boundaries. It's also easy because we're working with technology. I'm superhappy with all of my releases. It's like a chef working in a kitchen to perfect a dish…" Richie Hawtin's fascination with sake comes up for a moment. "What's so interesting is the starting point is exactly the same: it's rice. What you can get out of rice grains is incredible. I admire the thinking!"

I originally wrote this in two parts, as if it was a script for a movie, which in my head, it very much felt like. But of course, magazines don't work like that…

Looking back has actually been inspiring of late ("it's funny, a lot of that time has influenced my new album") but Rune's parents divorced when he was still young and he divided his time between the two of them "…and this is where I would go to feel free… I think the first freedom was in skateboarding. I really appreciate the magic of that time." After that, Rune started to play the drums and emulate what was being played on hip hop records: "But until someone told me the drums were sampled from old funk records, I couldn't figure out why they didn't sound like that! Immediately after that, my mum bought me an Amiga 500 and I started producing. And then after a while I got

CHAPTER TWELVE: FREETOWN CHRISTIANIA

into a radio show from a guy called Thomas [AKA Easy Cut] and would listen because of the hip hop he played but then through him would slowly get into the house thing. And the first time I heard The Goodmen – *Give It Up* and DJ Pierre – *What Is House Music*… these records made me think: why would I waste time making hip hop? And then I started making techno and house music. The first show I played was called The Youth House. People hated that music back then! It was a cool but dangerous time. My first record came out in 1995 on a label called Multiplex and then I started playing underground techno parties. I was so infatuated with this music, I felt like I had to tell everybody about it." The sensation he felt from the music, he says, was "like the first time you taste chocolate!"

A quick inspection of the vinyl in his studio confirms a reciprocal love of house and techno that effortlessly spans the past two decades: Daft Punk's *Discovery* and *Remedy* by Basement Jaxx mingle next to music and mixes from Carl Craig and Kenny Larkin and somewhere in the middle, you'll find a pristine pink copy of '95 Strictly Rhythm classic Lil Mo Yin Yang, AKA mid 90s super-duo Lil Louie Vega and Erick Morillo. "As a DJ, Derrick May was my biggest idol: you could feel it in the room. I also liked Jeff Mills but he wasn't as present when he performed. Later, when I went to Pacha to hear Erick Morillo… that was mind-blowing. The way he controlled the club was incredible."

Rune picks up the backstory again. "I fell in love in '96 and had my heart broken and then had a break until '99 when I did my first record for the Brother Brown guys. That was also the year I first went to Ibiza. The first trip was to San Antonio with a bunch of guys but what was beautiful was I found my way to Salinas to hear John Sa Trincha, who sold tapes back then! And then there was the resurgence of Cocoon and DC10 in 2003/2004 and that planted a seed which inspired me to make Ink and Needle records. And after Space, you would go from 8 in the morning until 5 or 6 in the afternoon!" He played Berghain for the first time in 2006 and finally adopted the Kölsch moniker as a solo artist in 2010. He signed to Kompakt on the suggestion of Michael Mayer, who insisted that his new moniker was his surname: Rune says his success couldn't have happened without the support and understanding of the label. His first release, the tough but richly melodic *Loreley*, paved the way for a slew of Kompakt Speicher club classics, and the 3rd artist album is due to drop in June.

"There's no such thing as being cool or underground," he says on the subject of club and crossover hits. "People sometimes downplay their musical skills, maybe because they don't have the talent to write anything better. All that music we regard as being cool from Chicago, the Dance Mania stuff: I was talking to K-Alexi a few years ago and he said they all wanted to make r 'n' b records but couldn't afford the equipment. They wanted to make pop, they just couldn't do it!"

Which leads us right back to where we started: to his early inspiration, to his parents, and to Christiania. Right now, he admits that he has "mixed feelings" about his place of birth. "It's a holding spot for lost souls and misguided ambition: it's so easy to drown yourself in that place and not go any further. I don't feel connected to it at all. I'll go visit my mum, because she lives right next to Christiania and hangs out there a lot." What do his parents make of his music? "My 'real' mum has been to many events over the years, including Roskilde. My dad remarried before he passed away, and my stepmother came to hear me play at Showcase in Paris and brought my aunt. All the kids were looking up at these grannies in the booth who went for it for five hours! I'd have loved my dad to have experienced this. He sadly passed away in 2003, just before I won a Grammy. He really wanted me to go back to school and study. It was either that or become a Buddhist monk, like him: they called him the Irish Catholic Buddhist because he would keep on preaching to anyone who would listen! Not that it matters, but there's always an element of wanting to prove yourself to your parents."

Our final stop-off is to a huge building where Rune played from 1994–98, when it was a heavyweight underground club. And while his own upbringing was undeniably more potent than my own, the fact that I'd been flown all this way to see where this artist had been his own first baby steps as a musician felt very special indeed and it's not surprising that we've stayed in touch since then more than ever, with Rune even guesting on my debut podcast which was recorded at Spiritland in Kings Cross back in 2020. We spent the best part of an hour nerding out about Blade Runner and Dune, which is, as any nerd will tell you, the best way to lose sixty minutes of your life. It's always a privilege when an artist opens up properly about their inner life.

"I used to come here as a kid and run around," he continued. "But in the 90s they put on techno parties. The problem was it would go on really late and as you can see, people live around here." We ask him how he feels to be back again on the eve of his 40th birthday. "Little details pop up. The mind has a tendency to remember fond memories, but there was also a lot of violence and shit going on back then. A lot of my friends aren't here now.

I'm just happy I escaped. I remember one of my friends saying, 'We don't have the talent that you have, but we all want you to succeed'. That's such an amazing thing to say to someone as a teenager: to recognise that someone can do something you can't. It's a very un-Danish thing to do."

It's also a truth that echoes across dance music culture from Christiana to Ibiza: wherever you're from, maybe true freedom is really only possible with the support of your friends."

It's very rare that a feature can write itself but having visited the hippy commune where Rune grew up and walked and talked while we stepped over ghosts and childhood memories, the true nature and core of what I needed to write came together beautifully and easily. Seeing and hearing the way he spoke and the fact he "escaped", it was clear that it was like any creative returning to their childhood roots to see how much it – or you – had changed. I was immediately struck by how pivotal this place was for the producer in front of me and the man I mostly knew via his music. Everything that happened since he was a boy can be traced back to this place and I innately understood why he'd invited me to fly over and see it. It's still a place I think about often.

CHAPTER THIRTEEN
ICE ICE BABY

If you'd told me at 21 that in my early forties I'd be flown to Iceland to interview Björk for a *Mixmag* cover feature, I'm not sure I'd have believed you—even if the whole trip took less than ten hours from start to finish and felt like something of a fever dream.

There are certain artists—often, it seems, female artists—who are very much "one of one." Living or dead, I'd say these include Aretha Franklin, Sade, Kate Bush, Christine McVie, Stevie Nicks, Amy Winehouse, and, near the top of the mountain, the former Sugarcubes singer and bona fide avant-pop icon Björk. I'd kept a close eye on her since she released her brilliant, Nellee Hooper-produced solo album *Debut* back in 1993. Her uncompromising vision has always been awe-inspiring to me.

As much as I am a fan of classic Madonna, I'm not sure I'd quite place her in the same "genius" category. However, borrowing a song Björk co-wrote called *Bedtime Story* in 1994 and making it her own with a video by Mark Romanek was a shrewd, near-masterstroke move of mid-'90s pop music. The germ of genius, though, lies in the song's main writer: Björk.

I'd never officially interviewed her during my five years at *Muzik* magazine, although I did manage to get her to answer a short album Q&A back when her record label was still called One Little Indian. She'd signed off the brief but sweet email with a single word: "warmth."

The closest I'd ever come to seeing her up close and personal was in the audience at her Royal Opera House show in 2002. It was a performance where the music of Mahler collided with what she'd later describe as "brutal" techno, and Benjamin Britten mingled with the atmospheric electronics of Matmos. Björk was augmented at one point by an Inuit choir, but the vision, the look, and the sound were all unmistakably Guðmundsdóttir—carved, naturally, out of ice.

But if I too was making my way up my own proverbial mountain, this crack-of-dawn flight from Gatwick Airport to Reykjavík for *Mixmag* felt like a testament to how far I'd come as a music journalist. We'd chipped away at this magazine cover concept for months, focusing primarily on Björk's new album *Utopia,* produced in collaboration with Venezuelan electronic producer Arca. As always, Björk was on the cutting edge, working with one of the most exciting production minds in electronic music. Mysterious and boundary-breaking, Arca was the perfect artistic foil, and the album turned out to be one of her best.

It was the perfect time to showcase and discuss *Utopia,* and I was thrilled. But every time I checked in with Björk's UK PR, Anna Meacham, it seemed like the timing wasn't quite right. The interview kept being moved—and then moved again.

And then, suddenly, there was news. Late on a Friday afternoon, the email came through: Could I catch a flight at 6 a.m. on Monday and do the interview face-to-face at 10:30 a.m.? There

CHAPTER THIRTEEN: ICE ICE BABY

would just be enough time for me to hear *Utopia* beforehand and then tell Björk what I thought of it. No pressure at all!

HOLY HELL was I nervous that day.

Before I flew, I'd asked Kölsch for his thoughts on Björk. He had this to say about her art, her direction, and her innate integrity:

"The first time I heard her was *Human Behaviour*—she was such a breath of fresh air. In Denmark, we have a lot of Icelandic people coming here, and it's kind of obligatory to go there too, so we have that connection. She was the first Icelandic pop star I'd ever heard of. *Hyperballad* and *All Is Full of Love* are my two favourites. I play *Hyperballad* all the time and even made a new version for my sets because the song is absolutely fantastic. I love the way she brought in Mark Bell in the mid-'90s; I considered him one of us. I was so impressed that she had an eye for that. And the Goldie connection was a big deal for me as well. She's still a big inspiration for me, even now! She's always incorporated art into her music—it's always been a tight-knit combination. To get close to that level of integrity is what we all strive for."

"Do you know what I like most about the title *Utopia*?" she asked me during our interview. "Everybody gets it straight away!"

Despite my initial nerves, the interview was going well from the get-go. I just needed to stop overthinking and focus on the present moment.

"In this time of Trump and Brexit, it's an emergency," Björk said. "I'm trying to think on a green level and what we're going to do about global warming. When Trump decided not to join the Paris Agreement, I was devastated. *DEVASTATED!* And I think what we're discovering now is that we will have to go really DIY and create the utopia ourselves. We need to recycle and grow vegetables! I also have a lot of faith in the next generation. We have 13-year-olds discovering ways to clear all the plastics from the ocean and biotech people growing fungus that can absorb CO_2. So I do believe we will find a way. There will be fewer animals, sadly, but the only way we're going to clean up the planet is with technology.

"I'm not saying I'm better than anyone else, but perhaps the role of musicians is to bring hope. And I think if the ten richest tech companies—Microsoft, Google, YouTube—each gave $1 billion, that's $10 billion to clean up the planet. That's what should be happening!"

We had one final ask for the print cover: would she, as a budding DJ herself, deliver a mix to coincide with her first *Mixmag* cover feature since the '90s? She was certainly a fan of DJ culture, and she still enjoys participating in it today, listening to the sounds of the class of 2024—including another *Mixmag* cover star, Shygirl, alongside Sega Bodega and footwork star Jlin.

She admitted to being a fan of "brutal, brutal, brutal" techno. "I've been DJing since I was a teenager—I just wouldn't call it that! I grew up in a town with 80,000 people in Reykjavík. If you wanted a good night out, you took over a bar, and that's what I've been doing ever since. You invite a group of friends—the smaller the bar, the better—and it's like your own party. And you don't have to clear up afterward!

"It grew and grew, and ever since I moved half my time to Brooklyn, I've been DJing there. We have a community of friends, and we have themes. One theme was basslines: me, Alex Ross, Brandon Stosuy, and David Longstreth from Dirty Projectors would get together at four in the afternoon. That would be my fantasy: to go to a second-hand bookshop, start on basslines, Bach cello concerts, drink coffee, and talk. That slowly developed."

Just before we went to press—remember, in 2017, *Mixmag* was still very much in print—the mix arrived digitally via Anna. Since I'd been on "Compiling Label Copy Duty" for the best part of 20 years, all I needed to do was dig out the original label copy for the mix from my archive. It was a genuinely incredible compilation of modern composers like Steve Reich and newer female producers like Kelly Lee Owens and Kelela. All of them must have felt like they'd been knighted by Iceland's reigning queen of electronic alt-pop—and to be fair, they sort of had.

And best of all? It featured BIRD SONG!

One person who has observed Björk's development from the very beginning is British musician Marius De Vries, a friend and collaborator who worked on her first triad of solo albums, as well as Madonna's classic *Ray of Light* album with William Orbit.

"She's restlessly curious," he told me over the phone from L.A., where—appropriately enough—he had been the Music Director on the Oscar-winning movie *La La Land*. I'd sought him out for this feature because it was clear they respected each other. As the interview came to a close, she even asked me to pass on her best wishes to him.

"She also interacts with current culture. To be part of her orbit is amazing. Leaving aside her songwriting, it's a combination of curiosity and fearlessness that helps define her. She has great artistic integrity and the courage to go where that leads. I watched her progression, finding her confidence and self-sufficiency. She's quick to learn and always had a sense that she needed to gain control of her destiny, especially as a woman in the music industry. And she's also a wizard on Pro Tools!"

If you've not heard the mix, I urge you to find it online—it's still one of the coolest projects I've ever had the fortune of being musically involved with. I'll always be proud that we brought Björk back to the pages of *Mixmag*. It showed how far the magazine had come since 2004 and 2005 in developing the leftfield-leaning ethos it has maintained ever since. The days of Moby and David Morales gracing the cover are long gone, but the credibility they represented remains important.

The current team, however, isn't interested in repeating past glories, especially with so many exciting new artists out there. Going back for the fifth time to someone pivotal like The Prodigy doesn't align with the magazine's forward-thinking mission. I'll never forget something brilliant that Jerry Perkins once said to me: *"We do not want to be the Mojo of dance music."* He was right, and it's a stance that brings us back to Björk and her *bird song*.

This is how we trailed it online:

"Perhaps the single most consistently creative and innovative artist on the planet, Björk has been immersed in and inspired by club culture since before her *Debut* in 1993.

Quite simply, she's an electronic music superstar.

Bjork's forthcoming album *Utopia*, co-produced by Arca with production one one track by Rabit, is a lush, emotional electronic affair. Her 40-minute mix – a global exclusive - is equally lush.

Here's what Bjork had to say about the mix:

"dearest music-lovers !

here is a little set for you .

it is most definitely flute and air themed and perhaps reveals the sonic environment my ears were in last year

I thank all the musicians . kindness , björk."

Even Resident Advisor, never knowingly generous or impressed with the efforts of other media, had nothing but good things to say – and we were bestowed our very first R.A. Mix Of The Day that month.

There was one final tick to achieve before we went to press. Bjork being Bjork, she'd requested a quick look at the feature before we went to press. It's a long way from the Muzik era, when artists would never see anything until it was in print, and a dodgy pull quote could start a feud that could last years. Even in the new era of collaboration with artists there's a reluctance to let the subject of a feature any control over the narrative. But frankly, Bjork is Bjork, and exceptions can be made. And there were no amends required. We just had a short message back; "I love it – girl power!"

Warmth!

Kindness

CHAPTER FOURTEEN
BACK TO THE BALEARICS

There are so many amazing covers and cover features from this era that it would be churlish not to mention some of the stand-out highlights. Once we decided that quality would be the main focus, rather than the generic wacky *Loaded*-style attitude I'd encountered when I first joined, the team gelled in much the same way *Muzik* had done twenty years earlier. Duncan Dick, now an extremely studious editor, and I arguably had a similar dynamic to Push and Ben Turner at *Muzik*. The magazine's reception each month from pundits, ravers, and industry insiders was a consistent joy.

Duncan explains: "My feeling was that, for a magazine to be relevant at that time, we had to think about what it could offer that social media—in particular—couldn't.

"I still believe that magazines are the best way to showcase photography and design, doing so in a way that a phone screen never can. So, we started to put even more emphasis on finding great photographers and then letting them express themselves. We put as much thought and creativity into ideas and talent for shoots—not just cover shoots—as possible. Whether it was finding a stuffed giraffe for Peggy Gou in a warehouse full of taxidermy in Hertfordshire; Björk surrounded by strange fruit and flowers à la the Renaissance portraits of Giuseppe Arcimboldo; Jeff Mills recreating his favourite movie, *Dark City*, on a Miami rooftop at 2 a.m.; Michael Bibi shot *chiaroscuro*-style in a pulsating crowd of dancers (in retrospect, an unfortunate choice for the issue that came out just as COVID kicked in); or traveling to a reclaimed open-cast coal mine in Germany to shoot Bicep halfway up a strange iron tower, we always aimed to create something unique.

"While, in theory, artists could now talk directly to their fans en masse via social media, I believed there was still a place for traditional journalistic skills—whether through proper interviewing, evocative and thoughtful description, or analysis of where an artist and their work fit within the context of the evolving scene. No dumbing down: write for people who read, and leave the rest to Instagram. We gave more latitude to writers to carve out their own style and express themselves. The research, effort, and skill that went into an artist feature were something artists clearly appreciated, and it was part of what made a feature in *Mixmag* a real career milestone.

"We had the opportunity to travel the world and showcase clubs and festivals that many of our readers couldn't experience themselves. We turned more of the magazine over to exploring scenes and parties—big and small—whether a communal rave in Turin or a festival held in the old *Star Wars* set in the Tunisian desert. We always paired these features with the best quality photography and writing, highlighting what was unique while also exploring the shared values across the scene and culture. For me, this was a far better use of space than reviews or even opinion pieces. Stan culture, tribalism, and oversaturation have diminished the value of reviews, while opinion is ubiquitous in the new media landscape—and 99.9% of it is probably not worth reading.

"But my biggest priority as editor was adding more diverse voices and talents to the magazine. Maybe it's because of the emphasis on work experience, or maybe it's just the way society is structured, but music journalism—and, indeed, all journalism—has long been a bit of a monoculture: the preserve of straight, white, middle-class men. That bias was reflected in our contributors (with no disrespect to them personally). By the time I took over as editor, you could add 'middle-aged' to that list as well.

"But that's never been representative of electronic music culture. We spent a lot of time finding new writers and photographers, particularly those local to the events and people we were reporting on. (I always hated the idea that you had to send someone from London to tell people about their own scene.) Using the same old stable of talent was certainly the easier, safer option—people who'd worked with us for years, who knew the style, the system, and had a reputation for reliability and quality. There was still a place for them.

"But the extra work in finding and nurturing new talent was incredibly rewarding, and, I think, to the massive benefit of the mag—especially in terms of new ideas and a broader insight into the culture. The online team at *Mixmag* had already started being proactive in diversifying the young people we got in as interns or for work experience. One thing I'll never regret was deciding that every single intern would get a session with me, explaining how the magazine was put together—from commissioning to layout to sub-editing, what everyone on the team's roles were, and where the opportunities might be for them. It also helped me evolve as an editor and a person. I remember: a) realising at one point that I'd often been more encouraging to interns who "reminded me of me" (hence the introduction of the formal mag sessions); and b) when one of the great new writers I'd found pointed out some lazy sexism in the generic brief I'd given to feature writers—cobbled together and added to over all my years at the mag. Some of the old attitudes had seeped in without me ever noticing. I was mortified to realise both of these things, and I'm still doing my best to make up for it."

And when you stand for something, the artists of note all come knocking because a *Mixmag* cover suddenly becomes something that you want on your wall alongside that head of a moose. In my eyes, in 2018 and 2019, and leading up to the lockdown especially, *Mixmag* could barely put a foot wrong creatively, and once the ideas started flowing, people really began to notice and want 'in.' *Mixmag*, as a magazine, was, according to the astute Jerry Perkins, the shop window to the brand, and everyone wanted to be behind that glass by the time we hit 2018. Best of all, with flowing ideas came stop-you-in-your-tracks covers: an iconic, glowing Dan Avery cover was shot by a former *NME* rock photographer named Steve Gullick, someone Ben Turner and Push would have surely worked with back in the mid-90s. In other words, the creative team was thinking outside of the box. Just as amazing was the Detroit techno pioneer Jeff Mills, who was interviewed by another long-serving *Mixmag* contributor, the erudite and always curious music writer Joe Muggs. Even now, it strikes me as a timeless cover, and there is an evocative accompanying shoot capturing the essence of Mills up close, by photographer Alexa Merico. The

CHAPTER FOURTEEN: BACK TO THE BALEARICS

magazine team had also been augmented by a smart young writer from Brighton named Jasmine Kent-Smith, someone I know our former production editor and now renowned nature writer Melissa Harrison hoped would one day become editor of the print title.

We've done quite a few 'Ibiza issues' over the years at *Mixmag*, but I do have a personal favourite of my own from 2018: interviewing the techno superstar Sven Väth, who was celebrating his somewhat surprising (and unusual) move to Pacha that season.

The cover image was shot by William Worrell, who had grown up on the island and, like myself, had been drawn in by the incredible, e-motional music on a Monday at Amnesia from Sven, Ricardo Villalobos, and their Chilean-Swiss production sparring partner Luciano, under the Cocoon umbrella. Before becoming part of the Cocoon crew, Will had been an art director at Jamie Jones' Paradise party during its early, formative years on the island. "I was in the right place at the right time," he said at the time, echoing something I'd long believed: all the best ideas happen after dark, and all the best connections are made under the stars. "A lot of my friends needed creative work done!"

Our day with Sven was also pretty special, a reminder that he and I share a similar mindset when it comes to music, art, and (when required) commerce—but with his own singular German vision, way ahead of anything I could muster from my comfortable sofa in Hackney. Sven first went to Ibiza in 1980 (!) and was immediately bitten by the Balearic bug, making the island his second home. Ironically, while I remember Cocoon parties happening at Amnesia in 1999 and 2000, the music seemed too dark and unrelenting for my young musical mind, which remained fixated on house music, until I suddenly noticed a switch from house to techno and minimal on the island around 2003 and 2004. This was when stencils of Sven as a pirate started appearing on walls around the island—a secret code for those in the know.

This change had been happening in tandem with Circo Loco at DC10, but Sven was the star attraction, and Ricardo Villalobos was his second in command on the terrace. And oh boy, what a brilliant pairing they were. Sven, the Teutonic techno metronome with a flavour and taste for adventure and dark melody; Ricardo, the more esoteric, wayward musical mind, with a love of Chilean percussion and records that often jumped as if they had a mind of their own (even though it was mainly misuse of plastic from overuse). If I think of this era, the record I remember best is Ricardo's singular remix of Depeche Mode's 'Sinner in Me,' a still-unreleased 15-minute remix masterclass that united the dancefloor in the same way that Sono's 'Keep Control' had done at Pacha and 'The Freaks Come Out' had done at DC10 for Luciano a couple of years later. But more than anything, this was an exciting place to be 24 hours a day, with beautiful European girls dressed for success, boys with bags of mischief in their shorts, and life-enhancing deep house everywhere you went. On a good day, the music wouldn't stop for 36 hours, and sometimes it would bleed into a second day on a beach or on a boat in the middle of nowhere. I miss those days without responsibility—and wouldn't trade those memories for anything.

For this 2018 cover, we'd decided to tour some of Sven's old haunts on the island, including Ibiza Town. "This represents my youth, when I was first here back in the '80s," he told me that afternoon. "By the port was the most important strip here. It was called 'the mile!' I found myself running around with my box of mixtapes from one bar to another. I was selling my mixtapes to three bars. One was called Graffiti, where I always had a gin and tonic in the evening. Later in the evening, you'd slowly cruise up the old town towards one corner where there was a bar called Dome. I think it still exists today, and it was where we all met before we went to the clubs. For me, the old town is the symbol of Ibiza. The evening always started there. Now it's all in Playa d'en Bossa."

Change is a recurring theme in my 25 years, so I asked him if Ibiza had changed. "Has Ibiza changed? It's a logical evolution," he replied pragmatically but beautifully. "Things are changing for good, and we've also improved. If you go up north to Sant Joan and places like this, you still have hippy communities there. They invite shamans to come from Mexico, Peru, and Brazil to do ayahuasca sessions. These people will never come to the clubs. You have your own little circles in the north, in the south, and on the other side, there's the hippy market still on. There is still that vibe. At Las Dalias, they still do these old-school Ibiza parties. It's not just about Bossa—there's much more to discover." So while you can sense Sven's reticence to embrace Bossa, there's no doubt that Ushuaïa and Hï had fairly revolutionised the clubbing experience on the island. It's more commercial, sure, and more of a show, but they know what they're doing, certainly in terms of the artists they work with. It was very telling that when David Guetta eventually left his 15-year-plus residency at Pacha, it was to join the Ushuaïa/Bossa team, and he remains there today with a new residency called (ahem) 'Future Rave,' with a young partner in crime named Morten. This season, his special guest over the summer was our *Muzik* favourite, the legendary Miami and

New York selector Danny Tenaglia, which can only be a good thing for a new generation to immerse themselves in musically.

Another clear cover favourite (and I always knew by how many people messaged us to say so) was the 2019 issue with the energetic Ninja Tune-signed Canadian house music producer Jayda G. She was shot by Rhys Frampton, and the image, taken at a daring and unusual angle, really made the magazine jump at you on the newsstand. Interviewed by another excellent new writer named Sirin Kale, with styling from Tori Amos' original '90s fashion stylist Karen Binns, this respected female selector had started to make waves with her music. But again, in the spirit of *Muzik's* halcyon mid-'90s era, *Mixmag* was now helping break artists out of their corner globally, with a magazine available at every airport and with a proper emphasis on the kind of fashion you'd normally only associate with *Essence*, *The Face*, or perhaps even *Vanity Fair*—in other words, it was confident and cool. We also returned to Jayda G again digitally with a feature written by yours truly, but I think the first cover was the one with the most impact. "There's something that is just kind of radiant about her," said Marea Stamp, AKA future cover star The Blessed Madonna, inside. "It's unmissable, and it makes you want to hear what she has to say."

Every month, the consistency remained, and it was so energising to see. *Mixmag* was weaving smart, music-driven life stories of a caliber I'd always dreamed of, and something I hadn't seen consistently at the title since I'd joined. Don't get me wrong, *Mixmag* had some brilliant covers over the years, including Daft Punk, OutKast, The Martinez Brothers, and future superstar DJ Maya Jane Coles back in 2011 (which was very early in her career), but then, for some reason, we'd swing back the month after with a feature about something silly. I have to give credit to the whole team in 2018 and 2019 – beyond our long-standing print Editor Duncan and myself, Art Director Hayden Russell, Senior Designer Vassilis Skandalis, Picture Editor Joe Plimmer (who I'd worked with 20 years before at *Muzik*), Digital Fashion Designer Lewis Munro, and *Mixmag*'s new Head of Digital, Seb Wheeler, with his then-number two (and now digital editor) Patrick Hinton – for aligning the needs of the new digital world with the still cutting-edge requirements of a magazine being sold in a slowly dwindling market.

While, by 2017, the once-important CD covermount mix had gone from being a physical card to an exclusive DJ mix you'd find online at Mixmag.net, that didn't mean they didn't pour their heart and soul into those one-hour mixes. The Jayda G mix, for example, opened with Fonda Rae's uplifting vocal disco vibes before coming to a close with *Call Me* by soul singer N'Dambi. In other words, it was becoming more important than ever to be seen as a bona fide selector. I should also give a brief shout-out to the hard-working fabric DJ and renowned author Bill Brewster, one of dance music's best writers and minds, who returned to *Mixmag* again and again to deliver great pieces in the front, middle, and back. As well as his superb Tensnake cover feature back in 2015, he also interviewed the UK fidget-house producer and former Major Lazer collaborator, Switch, in the same Jayda G issue. He had this to say about working with Chaka Khan: "Sarah Ruba and I wrote and produced everything with Chaka Khan," he said of her 2018 album *Like Sugar*. "I mean, she's a legend – and when she's in go-for-it mode, it's pretty spectacular.

It was nerve-wracking for me, even though I've been in the studio with very established artists before. Fortunately, Chaka is a real sweetheart, and one of my favourite people I've met of late." He also discussed working with Beyoncé and M.I.A., two artists I very much admire. But it's his St. Lucia story that I'm going to close with here. "I was working on the M.I.A. album in St. Lucia," he starts. "I was a gymnast when I was younger, although it's apparent that I am not as much of a gymnast as I once was. So, I took a dive off a cliff, broke a bunch of ribs, and knocked myself out. The people I was with had to jump in, fish me out, and resuscitate me."

I also spoke to *Mixmag*'s MD, Nick Stevenson, for the closing chapters of this book. His perspective, having worked at the brand for 22 years, is a reminder of his own and the brand's decades-long tenacity. "I never in my wildest dreams thought I'd ever get to work at *Mixmag*," he says. "In my first year of university, I was writing for a bunch of clubbing websites for free in my spare time. I used that experience as an excuse to apply for work experience at *Mixmag* in 2000. My two weeks there, via Editor Tom Whitwell, were two weeks that changed my life. After that, I kept in touch with as many of the staff as possible, bombarding them with ideas and showing my face in the office whenever I was in London. I became a regular freelancer, and the following summer, I was asked to be their staff writer in Ibiza for a season. That became four months that changed my life. The summer went so well, I started standing in for staff when they were away, and my Uni asked me if I still wanted a degree or if I just wanted to work at *Mixmag*. I was offered the staff writer job in the summer of 2002, so I went straight from Uni to *Mixmag*, where I've now been ever since – so that's 22 years – my entire adult life. And I continue to love every minute of it!"

"You've obviously progressed a long way from those early days," I point out. But for me, the long stint on Pentonville Road is a special one, and where *Mixmag* started to explore and run The Lab as well as early overseas franchises. "The secret as to why *Mixmag* has remained the market leader was most obvious during that time – its ability to adapt, to put journalism first, but always remaining fun. If I was being brutally honest, the other media brands in our field bore me to tears! Clubbing is fun, and *Mixmag*, at its best, always kept that level of humour and excitement in its output."

He understandably remains bullish about the new digital era. "*Mixmag* still prints magazines in numerous other territories; we have 22 *Mixmag* offices around the world, and many have retained the print mag, so it's technically still available around the world. For the UK mag specifically, the team has worked hard to transfer the authority, integrity, and humour of the print title across all our digital, social, and video touch points. And being digital-first means we're much less of a one-way street – the brand, at the need of its audience, has become more interactive and quicker to react. When I started at *Mixmag* in the early 2000s, we were celebrating our biggest issue selling 120,000 copies. Today, our global digital output has over 60,000,000 reach every month."

Duncan is also bullish about print as a whole: "It was my feeling that the future of the mag lay in creating a timeless, collectible product that people who loved the culture – and loved the brand – would be desperate to own. In fact, we were just about to launch a new redesign with better paper stock and a new emphasis on a subscription/membership model (it becoming quite clear that music magazines were becoming too much of a specialist interest for the likes of WH Smith, though specialist interests can still be pretty profitable) when suddenly we were all on furlough and the world stopped clubbing. I still believe passionately in the potential of print media and the music press: amid all the online noise, spam, and AI-generated guff, its authenticity will only stand out even more as time goes by."

These were the kinds of stories we now wanted to tell. Every single one of these issues remains in the archive!

CHAPTER FIFTEEN
(BECAUSE YOU GOTTA HAVE) FAITH

"Now is the time for everyone to stop non-essential contact and travel."

In March 2020, the United Kingdom collectively experienced something strange.

And we weren't the only ones—far from it.

The global outbreak of COVID-19 meant that the UK entered a national lockdown. Bumbling Prime Minister Boris Johnson was the man in charge, and many sectors of the market were forced to close, including all sectors of live entertainment. Of course, that meant my own sector—nightclubs, drinking establishments, and anything that remotely looked like a gathering or a festival—went dark. For how long, nobody could tell.

The slogan "Stay Home, Protect the NHS, Save Lives" was used in England, but despite the promise of a review every three weeks, lockdown trundled on. And it wasn't just nightclubs. Cinemas, theatres, concert halls, gyms, spas, and swimming pools were also affected. Some—particularly the movie-going business, which pivoted hard to cheaper, cushion-friendly home entertainment over lockdown—are still struggling to recover now. And nightclubs, the former homes of all manner of after-hour activity, came back into the light with a whole new focus and purpose. Some of these events were no longer called nightclubs: a new word crept in, and it's never left. The word is 'spaces,' and those spaces need to be safe, especially after a global pandemic.

It's been fascinating to watch, but not everybody made it: in 2023, *Trax Magazine* in France closed for good. *DJ Magazine*, however, resolutely remains in print. The only other print magazine of note was the return of Jockey Slut's excellent 90s magazine team with a new print publication called *Disco Pogo*. In many ways, their core values are more aligned with my own than ever, with covers ranging from Bicep, SHERELLE, and Gilles Peterson to Khruangbin and Elkka.

Closer to home, *Mixmag*'s killer print curation couldn't withstand the effects and repercussions of COVID. The UK print magazine closed in March 2021. The final cover featured breakthrough DJ star Michael Bibi, shot in chiaroscuro-style lighting amid a whirling crowd of ravers. The press of people pictured only served to remind us what we had lost with 'social distancing'. The magazine team was halfway through the next cover with NYC-based Korean shooting star Yaeji; copy written, cover shot. And, as with *Muzik* all those years ago, I know that pain of something special remaining undone, equal to the personal cost of losing what must count among the best jobs in the world.

Aside from the meltdown of the movie industry and watching nightclubs figure out how to monetise their four walls in the middle of super-strict restrictions, lockdown forced an issue we'd all seen coming but didn't know how to tackle. The market was changing, a new generation was about to arrive, and every rule we'd secretly written on tablets was about to be smashed to pieces. In short, dance music was suddenly about survival of the fittest. And sadly, despite a brilliant magazine team that included Duncan, Melissa Harrison, Deputy Editor and all-round good egg Sean Griffiths, plus long-standing art director Hayden Russell (who designed the cover of this book), *Mixmag* made the tough decision to close its main shop window.

A few months later, Nick Stevenson made the following announcement on the website:

"Firstly, we want to thank you for your valued support during a time of unprecedented industry turmoil. We're pleased to see some gradual easing of the lockdown, and some promising signs that we're all heading in the right direction. As you know, things are moving a little slower in the music industry as we find the safest way to bring back live music events. For the past 37 years, *Mixmag* has been bringing you the best dance content on the planet, which we are continuing to deliver on our website mixmag.net, as well as through all of our digital and social channels. But for now, we've made the decision to continue the temporary pausing of the publication. We want to thank you for your continued support of everything that we do."

The digital covers returned in October 2020 with issue 348. Pleasingly, DJ Yaeji was the first 'cover' back because I thought she set the tone for where *Mixmag* should be post-print: edgy, exciting, authentic, inventive—you name it, she had it. The New York-based producer had a look and a sound that was uniquely her own. Her musical agenda was also very refreshing: there was a more independent changing of the guard ahead, with a whole host of female artists coming through post-lockdown, sweeping away the middle and major (label) ground. "I used Ableton to arrange the tracks," she said. "Me and my laptop! Since social distancing has forced us to enjoy music in solitude, I've been putting together mixes on Ableton rather than recording it live on CDJs. I dug for new tracks (all but one track from Bandcamp) specifically for this mix," she continued. "Queer/POC artists only. I made this mix with the same excitement as wanting to share good music I just found with a close friend."

After Yaeji, we championed the likes of Romy, TSHA, and Shygirl on the now-digital fortnightly cover, and that spirit of celebrating the new and fresh continues today editorially. I don't think *Mixmag* has ever been as cutting-edge as it is now in its long history.

Around the same time, Defected Records in London decided to bring back London's two-decade-strong acid house bible, *Faith Fanzine.* For the first issue, I interviewed Danny Tenaglia and Harry Romero in conversation together for the cover (and yes, it was conducted via Zoom—a word I'd soon come to shudder at when it came to meetings over lockdown). *Faith* celebrated all things "HOUSE!" for a generation that had grown up on Frankie Knuckles, Lil Louis, Farley and Heller, DJ Harvey, and all things Chicago—which, in part but not entirely, was a bit of me. Once that returning issue with Danny and Harry had been "put to bed" (as we always described the last day of deadline at *Muzik* and *Mixmag*), I had another possible cover idea: an interview with the all-round English music legend Paul Weller for the next issue.

Over at Universal Records, my friend Tom March, the former Darling Department press champ, was now the co-president of Paul Weller's long-standing UK label, Polydor. (*Quite the jump from junior press officer at The Darling Department!*) Tom agreed that with recent *Faith* covers ranging from Four Tet and Cassy to

CHAPTER FIFTEEN: (BECAUSE YOU GOTTA HAVE) FAITH

Honey Dijon, and with me in the interview hot seat, this was a cool and intriguing look for Paul. While Weller inevitably found his way into *The Times* and *The Guardian* with every returning interview, he was rarely discussed in house music circles, even though he'd covered *Promised Land* as a member of The Style Council and closely followed the evolution of acid jazz in the early '90s. He also dressed sharper than a brand-new Stanley (Road) knife and was once married to the ultra-stylish soul singer DC Lee, who had also been in Wham! in their early days. There was plenty to talk about musically, even if he wasn't the type to sit at home scouring Discogs for Drexciya records on a Monday night.

Like many acid house heads, I was also a long-term fan of his music. I may have been too young for The Jam, but I was the perfect age for *Wild Wood, Sunflower,* and especially the lovelorn single *You Do Something to Me*, which revealed a soulful sensitivity missing from so many of those mid-'90s pretenders like Cast, Shed Seven, and Menswear. Still, I was wary because I knew Paul doesn't like looking back and doesn't suffer fools gladly. However, he's released a new album every 18 months or so for a long time, so we had a product to plug. The eventual answer was yes—result!

The following snippet of the interview should show why I have such fond memories of my one-hour Zoom chat with Paul.

"I always see music in terms of pictures," he said early on when I asked if he connects or considers music as akin to painting in terms of creativity. "When I'm writing and I start a song, I get this picture emerging in my mind, and I think there's definitely something coming from a similar source."

Before the chat, I had asked Irish DJ/producer and legendary music supervisor David Holmes a question via email for Paul.

David said he admired "Paul's constant reinvention as an artist and his curiosity for new music." Where did that come from?

"I keep myself on my toes! Like a boxer, you've got to be on your toes! I don't think you can ever stop learning, no matter what it is," Weller replied. "It's foolish to think you know everything there is to know. My wife always takes the piss out of me because I believe in magic and I think magic is real, and she always says, of course, it's not. Well, even if it isn't, none of us can prove that—and what am I gaining by not believing it? So I guess that's where I am coming from. I'm not someone who got into their 40s and thought their best years were behind them."

I asked Paul for an example of something magical to close.

"I don't want this to sound flashy, but that happens almost every single night! I'm extremely lucky to feel that it happens almost every night!"

As a result of this interview, the Pet Shop Boys ended up remixing Paul's next single, *Cosmic Fringes*, over lockdown. I was happy to have helped make this happen by mentioning that I'd assisted the band with remixes of their singles and connecting Neil with Paul afterward. The remix was excellent, clocking in at around ten minutes and clearly inspired by Chris Lowe's early love of Donna Summer and Giorgio Moroder. Much like Carl Craig's equally epic and radical remix of *Inner Sanctum* (which the PSBs proudly sold on 12-inch vinyl at their Royal Opera House shows), Paul also pressed physical copies of *Cosmic Fringes* for his musically curious core fan base. Neil even added his voice subtly in the mix, as he had done before on their superb remix of Madonna's *Sorry*.

In other words… magic.

CHAPTER SIXTEEN
LAZARUS

Twenty-five years is a long time in anyone's book, but this book just happens to be mine.

Looking back, it's clear that sometime in my early twenties, my (teenage) hobby became my proper job. Fortunately, 25 years later, my full-time job continues to be my all-time favourite pastime. There's rarely, if ever, a day when I'm not "on," and there's never a day I resent spending in my inner sanctum, listening to music—whether it's house, jungle, techno, hip-hop, or the latest orchestral suite from Erland Cooper or Robert Ames & Ben Corrigan.

But I remain a big believer in roots.

When I was a child, my mum would take me to see the latest Hollywood blockbusters in Burgess Hill. I can still vividly recall seeing R2D2 and C3PO traverse the deserts of Tatooine during *Star Wars,* the crack of Indy's whip in *Raiders of the Lost Ark,* and the soaring John Williams score that underscored the unbelievably moving *E.T.* in 1982. All these movies burrowed deep into my brain before I was ten-years-old.

The two years I spent working at my friend Steve's independent Burgess Hill store, Round Sounds (originally part of a chain called Rounder Records with stores in Worthing and Brighton), were instrumental in my understanding of music. I absorbed catalogue numbers, learned which labels boasted the biggest and best artists (Warner had Madonna and Prince, EMI had The Beatles, and during Britpop, Coldplay, Radiohead, and Blur), and developed a definitive grasp of rock, pop, and dance music. I did my 10,000 hours—and then some! So, thank you, Steve, and to everyone who endured us when all you wanted to do was buy a single by someone we didn't particularly like.

In January 2016, I asked my mum if she wanted to see the brand-new *Star Wars* movie starring Daisy Ridley (and most of the original cast) with me. I even broke a two-decade habit and returned to Burgess Hill cinema. Steve's record shop was long gone, and the town center was fairly decimated, but it was a lovely experience to share with my mum. It also gave her the chance, for the umpteenth time, to ask if Harrison Ford was still married to Calista Flockhart.

Before the film, an advert popped up for David Bowie's new album, *Blackstar*. I quietly turned to my mum and said, in my best music critic's voice, that he was England's greatest living songwriter.

We both enjoyed our return to the wars of the stars, and afterward, I returned home to Hackney. I have a nice photo of my mum from that day: she looks over the moon.

Two days later, at around eight-thirty in the morning, my phone rang—unusual even in my house.

It was Mum, calling from Chichester. She sounded like she had something to say, but I'd already heard the news on 6 Music earlier that day.

"It's Mum, dear. David Bowie has died!"

CHAPTER SIXTEEN: LAZARUS

The death of David Bowie felt like the departure of a North Star from my youth. I wasn't alone in that feeling—the ripples of his passing are still felt today. The only other artist whose death hit me as profoundly was the irrepressible acid house producer Andrew Weatherall. Prince was another taken too soon. And the fourth would have to be George Michael. All were cruelly gone within the same two-year period. These were uncompromising artists, with musical destinies they directed and fulfilled. But Bowie's death felt sadder to me than any member of the royal family's ever could.

Later that evening, I went out for a drink with the Pet Shop Boys. The plan had already been arranged with their keyboard player, Chris Lowe, but now Neil wanted to join us too. We met at a quiet bar on the corner of Hoxton Square, where they talked about their experience of working with Bowie and what he had meant to them. It's an evening I will never forget.

It was also a reminder of how much my mum understood what music—and its main protagonists on stage—meant to me.

On June 20, 2023, my own mother passed away peacefully.

She'd hinted at her imminent departure during our last call. I was in the park near my flat, and I just knew.

"How are you doing?" I asked.

"Not so good, dear," she replied.

For the next few minutes, I thanked her for everything she'd done for me, my voice close to breaking but holding it together. I shared a lighthearted anecdote about *We Are The World* involving Bob Geldof. And then we were done.

We never spoke again.

I'm writing this final chapter one year after Mrs. Moore's departure from the planet. At her funeral, our loyal school friend

Maggie Kear delivered a brilliant eulogy that has stayed with me ever since: *"She never raised her voice, except to sing."*

She's now floating out in the cosmos somewhere, alongside her favourite foil, Jon Fielder, who is reportedly writing a new musical—hoping David Bowie might consider a brief cameo. Andrew Weatherall has already volunteered to DJ the after-party at the cosmic club's finale, but only if he can play pure rockabilly. Payment isn't necessary, though he might accept new brogues if pressed. It all promises to be, quite literally, out of this world.

Aside from being a big believer in roots, I'm also a firm believer in good endings—likely the influence of the film and book lover in me.

So here are some things I've learned.

In the pre-social media era of what we now call one-way media, traditional press officers and roving PR teams were the absolute gatekeepers of the music industry and its stars. That is, unless you managed to strike up a genuine friendship with the artist after an interview or during a few days on the road—something that, I'll admit, happened to me once or twice.

Today, however, the story of an artist's journey feels more like a jigsaw puzzle. It's not just about gracing the cover of *Mixmag*, a mix via Boiler Room or landing a "Mix of the Day" on *Resident Advisor*. It's about connecting these moments to create a broader narrative—a fully formed picture of the artist—rather than simply spending an afternoon doing promo before moving on to the next agenda item.

Take, for example, the lovable British junglist Nia Archives. Her rise has been a carefully assembled mosaic: an early *Mixmag* Lab session, a *Mixmag* digital cover, appearances on *The*

CHAPTER SIXTEEN: LAZARUS

Face cover, and even *The Evening Standard's* Friday magazine. Each piece of her promotional puzzle told a different story. I also had her on my two-hour *Worldwide FM* show, where she spoke with equal passion about Grace Jones and Dot Cotton from *EastEnders*.

Another moment of truth.

One of the biggest changes since 1999 is the level of access artists provide—or, more often, don't provide. Today, an artist's Instagram account can wield more impact than giving fifteen minutes to *MTV*, *BBC2*, or even *Channel 4 News*.

Try asking any senior press officer for time with a top-tier artist. Forget icons like Björk or Madonna; even getting thirty minutes with Peggy Gou or Justice is tough unless it's for a prestigious cover feature. The days of spending almost a week on the road with an artist, "for colour," as I did with Underworld for my first feature in *The Times,* are long gone.

Some artists, as we've seen over the past decade, thrive on aloofness and mystery. No matter how hard we try, it's unlikely that Richard D. James—aka the musical genius Aphex Twin—will ever grace the cover of *Mixmag*. Similarly, Fred again.., arguably the most impactful and ticket-selling electronic artist of his generation, appeared on *Mixmag's* cover once but has since become such a global force that he no longer needs to engage with traditional press outlets, whether *The Times*, *The Face*, or *i-D*. Even Four Tet, who has never particularly cared for "traditional" dance music press, now feels more aligned with the *Pitchfork* audience.

And that's okay. The only constant in this fast-moving digital landscape is change.

Today's promotional journey is more like stitching together a patchwork quilt. An early *Mixmag* digital cover, blasted to over a million Instagram followers, is part of the puzzle, but it's no longer the whole picture. You need streaming playlist support—lots of it. Some love from *The Face* or *i-D*. Attention from BBC Radio 1 helps, but an Essential Mix or Essential New Tune won't guarantee a major label deal anymore. These days, it's about going viral and, crucially, maintaining consistency in your music releases. Waiting four years between projects? That's no longer an option.

For music journalists in 2024, writing is probably one of many things you do—not the only thing. Unless you're fortunate enough to be on staff, writing the odd thousand-word feature each month won't pay the bills, and the hustle is real. Longevity in the industry, whether as a journalist or a DJ, requires careful navigation. Consider multi-genre DJ Arthi Nachiappan, a Warwick graduate who, despite selling out shows across Europe and seeming to "smash it" on the surface, until recently held down a day job as a business news presenter for Sky TV.

One title and brand that's navigating this evolving media landscape is *Disco Pogo*. As I wrapped up this book, I spoke to promoter and editor in chief Johnno Burgess for insight.

"In 2019, Paul Benney and I started a *Jockey Slut* Instagram, posting old articles and building a community. We gained a couple of thousand followers quickly," Johnno shared. "We wanted to do a magazine about Andrew Weatherall, using vintage articles—a bit like those thick *Q Magazine* specials. Then Andrew passed away a month before the pandemic. With time on my hands, the Weatherall tribute book evolved from that. It sold 9,000 copies and could have sold more, but we stopped there.

CHAPTER SIXTEEN: LAZARUS

"It made us realise the lasting resonance of *Jockey Slut*. People like David Holmes and Jeff Barrett still talked about it with affection. Over the pandemic, there was a renewed interest in physical products—books, T-shirts, tangible things you could hold. That success gave us the idea to revive the brand with a Crowdfunder for a bi-annual magazine. However, the name *Jockey Slut*, which worked in the '90s, became misconstrued over time. It originally reflected obsession—like being a trainspotter for DJs and tunes—but now sounded sleazy. So we rebranded as *Disco Pogo*, a tagline from the original magazine."

What advice does Johnno offer aspiring young music writers?

"Modern fanzine writers are content creators now. That's your way to gain access to artists, support them, and get into parties and festivals for free, as we used to with magazines. Content creation is tricky to get right. At Mighty Hoopla, for example, we have a brilliant person who nails the tone and wording. It's similar to learning the house style of a magazine or newspaper.

"Having said that, festivals like London's *Wide Awake*, which attracts a more esoteric, indie-leaning crowd, might embrace physical print fanzines to reflect their individuality."

Perhaps the most interesting aspect of our conversation revolves around making it work financially. "On the original Crowdfunder, we set the target at £40k but ended up raising £60k, which was obviously amazing. We then realised we had to do a great job. We decided on a bi-annual schedule because it's not a full-time job for any of us. We aimed at an older demographic, probably aged 35-60, and for people who still enjoy long-form articles. It's almost like a bi-annual book, something people save for a summer holiday, to read over a week.

We decided to pay a competitive rate per word. We've lured writers we deeply admire, like Craig McLean and Andrew Harrison, and when their copy comes in, it's incredible. That sets the tone. We're also influenced by *The Word*, which was an exceptional magazine. My heroes include Mark Ellen, who edited *The Word*, *Q*, and *Smash Hits*. I'm a product of *Smash Hits* myself. Mark has spoken about being an 'amateur' in those early '80s years, and that's not a criticism—it's a spirit. Back then, you'd somehow get Sting's number, call him up, go over for tea, and get the interview done, partly because no one knew the 'professional' process.

Jockey Slut was born out of that spirit—it was amateur hour, but the passion was there. *Disco Pogo* still operates like a posh fanzine. If we want to devote eight pages to one amazing record, we can. For our Grace Jones cover, her musical director Ivor Guest spoke to us, and from there, we could choose contributors we admire, like Alexis Petridis writing about her disco era. It's a privilege to do that.

It's a labour of love—and it's led to books. Our Daft Punk book has sold 5,000 copies, so financially, we've found a way to make the overall business work."

Mixmag remains *Mixmag*, and *DJ Magazine* remains *DJ Magazine*, but neither wields the influence they had at their peak, when they were selling 100,000 copies in print. This isn't particularly controversial: *Mixmag's* recent pivot to digital was both a choice and a necessity during lockdown. However, its current demographic (ages 18-26) doesn't voraciously buy print publications as my generation did in the '90s and 2000s. Today, everything comes via smartphones, and the news needs to be snappy, ideally in bite-sized soundbites.

CHAPTER SIXTEEN: LAZARUS

I love *Mixmag's* emphasis on high-quality covers featuring leftfield artists. Many of these artists—like Shygirl, Romy, and Fred again…—have gone on to become bona fide ticket-sellers of the highest musical caliber.

Being part of the conversation is key. When SHERELLE was shot on horseback for the cover in October 2021, it took a lot of preparation, but the result was iconic in every sense of the word. The interview was a statement of intent, and SHERELLE has brilliantly united figures like Mary Anne Hobbs and I. Jordan along the way. In her own words: "I wanted Pete Tong to be at home listening to it like, 'Jesus fucking Christ, who the fuck is this?'" She was awarded Essential Mix of the Year for that blistering two-hour set, so clearly, he was.

It's worth noting that the digital cover came after an incredible viral Boiler Room moment, which catapulted her to the next level. I'm proud that *Mixmag* has managed to secure quality time with Björk. In 2018, she gave us a serious chunk of her time, and the accompanying mix (with birdsong!) remains one of our biggest DJ mix coups. Similarly, Fred again…'s exclusive mix for us now lives on Apple Music.

Over the past 25 years, I've been fortunate enough to meet most of my heroes. When I'm in a room with Depeche Mode, John Frusciante, or William Orbit, I just need to be myself, do my homework, and focus on their latest project—whether it's an album, a label, or even a new painting. I've distilled everything I've learned over the years: showing genuine passion for what I do is usually enough of an icebreaker.

Do your homework. That advice remains as true now as it was in 1994. Be open to the right frequencies.

Radio has become a new frontier for me. Lockdown made artists more available, with no touring schedules to manage. Suddenly, Curt Smith from Tears for Fears, Noel Gallagher, and Martin Gore from Depeche Mode had time to chat. Radio is its own community. Stations like Worldwide FM bridged gaps during COVID's darkest moments. One DJ, Luke Unabomber, united Balearic heads with sets that spanned The Brand New Heavies to Crooked Man.

Now, as I finish this book, I'm embarking on a new journey with Voices Radio in King's Cross. I'm not sure if it reaches as far as West Sussex, but I plan to play a lot of Prince. After that, I might take my first sabbatical.

Would I recommend someone pursue a lifelong career as a music journalist in 2024? I'm not sure. So much has changed in three decades. The pandemic essentially reset the industry, causing many mid-tier careers to fall through the cracks while newcomers reassessed the agenda.

There's more demand for content than ever, but less willingness to pay for it. Our attention spans are shorter, yet the allure of a deep dive on a favourite artist remains timeless.

Opportunities to become the next Amelie Lens or Charlotte de Witte are rare—but that doesn't mean you shouldn't try. A meaningful life in music is a dream if you can make it work.

Whether you can survive on Spotify or Bandcamp royalties is another conversation entirely.

So here's my advice: find your community, figure out how to be useful within it, and always be open to the right frequencies.

EPILOGUE

Some of the people I've worked with or known are no longer with us.

The first big shock for me was the death of Cassius producer Philippe Zdar, who tragically passed away in 2019 at the age of 52 after an accidental fall from a window—far too young. Philippe had mixed a CD for me at *Muzik* and later did so again during my early tenure at *Mixmag* when it was based on Pentonville Road. After delivering the mix—despite some very last-minute clearances needed on my side—he sent me the hour-long WAV file with a note that read, "We make a good team."

Ben Kouijzer, died even younger, at just 36. Ben was a brilliant and beloved agent at CAA UK, representing acts like 808 State, Harry Romero, Craig David and The Orb. He passed away from kidney and liver failure after bravely battling cancer. Ben was originally diagnosed with a malignant peripheral nerve sheath tumour (MPNST) and underwent surgery and radiotherapy, only to learn that the cancer had metastasized to his lungs.

Ben and his fiancée, Lotte Bowser, relocated to Tijuana, Mexico, in search of treatment. Tragically, he tested positive for COVID-19 in late October, and a combination of factors led to kidney and liver failure. He passed away in the early hours of a Sunday morning. Lotte said afterward, "We are beyond devastated. We are all hurting together."

Ben's legacy is lovingly upheld by Lotte, who is now writing a book about her time with this remarkable man. I was proud to call him a friend. It seemed like Ben and Lotte were beginning to map out a life together here in East London, making his death in Mexico an even greater tragedy. Ben was a kind, passionate man who loved music deeply, and his global team at CAA continues to honour him. He will not be forgotten.

Closer to my day-to-day community was Shaun Roberts, for many years the heart and soul of *fabric*'s Friday nights as a booker and promoter. I recently wrote a short piece for fabric about Shaun ahead of the club's midweek charity fundraiser with The Chemical Brothers, Daniel Avery, and others, held to support his fight against colon cancer. Here's an excerpt:

"I lived in *fabric* for 15 years," Shaun said, keen to shift the focus away from himself and toward raising awareness of a medical issue that remains under-discussed. "The club is a huge part of who I am. Without it, I wouldn't have met most of the incredible people who've been supporting me over the past few weeks. It's a testament to the community that has grown around Charterhouse Street and to the people who steer it. Offering to host a fundraiser for me at the venue is such a generous thing to do, and I really am honoured.

"And now we have this quite ridiculous lineup of artists, many of whom I'm proud to call friends. It's going to be very emotional. Is it OK to wear sunglasses in a club if you're crying?"

Shaun Roberts' family confirmed that he passed away on Christmas Eve (December 24), 2022, after bravely battling colon cancer since 2019. Shaun's brother, Marc Roberts—a well-respected promoter and father himself—described him as: "a ferocious, brave warrior until the very end. But your body could only take so much, and you knew it was time to go. Thank you for hanging in there so we could make it back to say goodbye—for which I will be eternally grateful."

Like Ben, Shaun made an indelible impact behind the scenes, and his contributions were nothing less than first class.

As for me, I've been fortunate to have a ringside seat in rave culture, witnessing its fortunes ebb and flow. I will always be grateful for that, particularly in iconic hubs like London, Paris, Berlin, Miami, and Ibiza.

I've watched Annie Mac rise from her early days being featured in the pages of *Mixmag* to becoming a bona fide broadcasting legend, a heavyweight festival draw, and now a published author. A core memory for me is hearing her sign off her last-ever Radio 1 show with the haunting strings of Rolando's instrumental Detroit techno classic, *Knights Of The Jaguar*. I also fondly remember decompressing with her after a show in Ibiza, chatting about music and life while listening to Donna Summer's *State of Independence* on her Pacha hotel balcony. She remains an inspiration for the new generation of emerging female DJs.

I've marvelled as David Guetta's career evolved—from his early days on the Space terrace in a simple white vest to his now-famous Thursday nights at Pacha in Ibiza. I've spent hours talking about music with Fatboy Slim and Armand Van Helden, then watched them DJ together in a boxing ring at Brixton Academy—where Norman Cook won, just. I've seen Sasha drop his spine-tingling instrumental classic *Xpander* on the Courtyard at Cream in Liverpool and watched the place erupt.

I've had surreal moments, too—like meeting Beyoncé on tour in South Africa with Paul Oakenfold. It was back in 2004, at an event honouring Nelson Mandela called *46664*. I even got Beyoncé's autograph for my niece! I was lucky to get the much-loved BBC presenter and selector Annie Nightingale to share a chart of her current club favorites for *Faith Fanzine* just before she, too, departed this realm.

Before writing—and now finishing—this book, my biggest assignment in hardback was contributing a 10,000-word feature for the Pet Shop Boys' fan club book, *Annually*. Chris Heath was away, and the duo wanted a deep dive into their formative dance influences—a topic I happen to know inside and out! When my number one contemporary pop culture writing hero emailed me after reading the piece, I was walking on air for the rest of the week.

I dug out that email before writing this part because it highlights the importance of stopping to appreciate the small victories. Even this short message from Chris Heath was written with a level of precision most of us can only dream of. It was a reminder that, no matter how long you've been in the game, a little support and assurance can go a long way.

"Ralph,

Hi. Just wanted to say how well I thought your [PSB] conversation and article turned out - it had just the right combination of intimacy and back-and-forth and history. Thanks again for doing it, and also for turning it around swiftly over the holidays, especially given the on-going chaos surrounding us all.

Best wishes,

Chris"

The only constant is change. In the end, it all comes down to community, and I'm privileged to be a part of this one.

Mum, I hope I made you proud up there!

ACKNOWLEDGEMENTS

I would like to thank Mr Pete Chisholm (MBE) who also helped me navigate institutional racism so effectively as a green/blue teenager and to Judy Blume's book 'Forever' for breaking the ice with girls from the get-go. I owe you all bottles of something fancy for sure! To David Trethowan (R.I.P.) for threatening us with the cane but keeping us in check while being Cuckfield's answer to Darth Vader and to Brian Webb for comic relief from '88 onwards. And to Rebecca Bradley and her twin sister Victoria for saying such kind things about Mum ("Mrs Moore!") as I finished this book.

To my own family past, present and future: my sister Elena and Will Sheward, Danny Thomas, Cherelle, Antonella and Hayden Thomas and their respective partners and children Valle, Solly and Lola: Catford's circle of life continues.

To Mum's friends Will and Alf for inviting us to Bromley and keeping things Optimus in my childhood prime: a beautiful Boxing Day memory and the best Christmas present I ever received as a Transformer-obsessed kid.

To George Lucas and Steven Spielberg for *Star Wars*, *Indiana Jones* and especially for *American Graffiti* – I wouldn't be me without any of these IPs or characters. And to David Lynch for directing *Dune* over *Return Of The Jedi* back in '84: you made the right decision and it amuses me to this day.

To Stan Lee for being the only person to make my hand shake with pure adrenaline in LA and to Spider-Man co-creator Steve Ditko for writing back to my fan letter just before he too passed into the next realm: Marvel-ous, priceless, full circle memories.

To Kate Bush for a lifetime of digging and Tori Amos for all the precious things

To Duncan Dick for editing this 70,000 word piece of work into proper shape ("3 things!") and to Colin at Velocity Press for countering my original book idea with this one, which was much better.

Inner Sanctum shouts to Neil Tennant and Chris Lowe, Stuart Price, Angela Becker and Charlie Coletta, the original Acetate family: the peerless and fearless Shrina Lakhani, Maarten Puddy and Alice Morris, to Joshua and the extended Hampstead crew, Naomi Cambridge and Serena Sharp Singh, Rosh Singh and Cassius Sharp Singh, Roddy + Ann Sutherland and family, Emily Pritchard and Chana Joseph, Ailsa Kerr and Ben Clarke, Tom March, Nancy and family, Kelly and Mark Ralph and family, Helen and Lucy Coates and family, Lisa Larn and Jai, Sangheeta Lengar for the taco support, Sarah Qaiser + Johannes Goller, Ayelet Hacohen + her beautiful fam, Yvette Redmond for the constant career cheer-leading, the amazing 'This Is Your Life' book and for keeping my library colour-co-ordinated and my work books tidy, to Dean Richmond and family and to anyone who danced at Rock Cottage back in the day, to John Storer, Clare Coultas + Lyra Coultas-Storer, Dean Driscoll and Frida, Ed and Marika, Doug and Jef Ker, Sam Schindig and Andrew Ward, Michelle Sanchez and last but not least to Miss Stephanie Paul.

West Sussex shouts to Jon Fielder's sparring/life partner and de facto manager Maggie (Hathaway) Kear in Balcombe for endless enthusiasm and to all my friends from school for going the distance for 35 years: Stephen Brewer, Scott Rolling, Ben Potts and David Cobbett and their respective partners and extended families. To Steve Jackson and Ian Livingstone for keeping me in the world of Allansia from the corner of my Burgess Hill bedroom: my Stamina and Skill remains strong! To my post-Cuckfield college crew: Allison Heath/Griffin + fam, Kathryn O'Donnell, Doug and Stella, Martyn Armitage and the original Barcombe massive with mid '90s music shouts to Simply Red, Prince and Suede and to the much-missed Brighton Centre Record Fair crew. To Hannah Norrie for taking me to the 'Discotheque' and to David Bowie for Tin Machine, 'Hello Spaceboy' and 'I Can't Give Everything Away'.

To everyone who played a part in my Wonder Years at Warwick University: Russell Davis ("did we go?") and his always planning ahead endeavors as well as Emmie and JJ and Alison Davis. To Anna Howard, Chris Kirsch, Chris Miller and everyone who came through the door and stayed in Leamington Spa, Helen Broadway (we did the triple!), James King and Stephen Merchant (whatever happened to them?) and to Music 365 for letting me play Snoop Dogg and Dinosaur Jr. on the radio airwaves on a Saturday afternoon. And especially to the Warwick Boar - still going strong! And for featuring my early print interviews with One Dove, Paul Oakenfold, BT and The Charlatans: I have all these on file too. To the incredible artists who all came to Warwick during their respective runs: The Orb, Primal Scream, The Charlatans, Skunk Anansie, Todd Terry, Fluke, Sister Bliss and Pete Cunnah of D:Ream. And to Dolly Clew, formerly of Virgin Records and now a kick-ass photographer for always supplying me out with t-shirts in the early years.

Italy '95 with *Clerks* and *Quiz Show* & Tribal Gathering with Orbital + Hawtin

Let's get physical!

East London shouts to everyone else who made their mark in the past twenty-five years in the printed electronic music press: '98 and '99 IPC Media Muzik shouts to Ben Turner and Frank Tope for believing in me and getting me that life-changing staff writer position, to Andy Crysell for writing what I still think is the definitive Sasha artist feature in *Muzik* (I hear there is a book on the way!), Rob da Bank and Karen Young, Push from *Electronic Sound* for being so generous with his time and thoughts for this book, Rebecca Walters down in Fulham, Cathy Bell, James Barton, Rich McGinnis, Darren Hughes, Calvin Bush for the early Muzik album review support, Tom Mugridge and Thomas H Green for the Stetson sensibility, Duncan Bell, Malik Meer and to all of the PRs in the outside world who made things happen, especially Shane O'Neil at East/West and Island Records, Ruth Drake and Beth at Toast PR, Eden Summers and the Beat Hotel crew, Jasper Watkins and all at Southbank, Paul Guimaraes and his ace Periodic DJ posters, Indy Vidyalankara, Barbara Charone/MBC PR, Murray Chalmers PR, Jack Beadle, Erol Alkan + Iraina Mancini, Miss Kittin, Carl Cox, Steve Angello, Sebastian Ingrosso and Axwell and everyone else who provided CD-DJ mixes. To Ed Cartwright and the original Darling Department team especially Tom March and Jon Wilkinson. To James Pitt and Hayley, Lottie, Sophie Lloyd, Rowena Jones and Zoe Prothero – you know who I am and where I live. To Caroline Prothero and Myd and all those crazy Parisian producers, to Helen Smith/McGuire + her extended fam, Kaye Smith and anyone else who remembers what Dalston looked like 20 years ago and last, but not least, to Martin Gontad (between you and me) who knows what the dance music landscape looked like 25 years ago and continues to shape it in South America.

To The Word's core writing + wider marketing team: Andrew Harrison, Alex Gold, Mark Ellen and David Hepworth, Kate 'Whoops Now' Mossman and Fraser Lewry for the stories and XFM Polaroids.

And for the past twenty years of Mixmag, Pacha Magazine and Faith Fanzine: Pauline Haldane (where are you now?), Gavin Herlihy and Laura Jones, the always inspiring Melissa Harrison and Scout, Peter Rogers, Sean Griffiths, Patrick Hinton, Megan Townsend, Katie Scrafton and Juliet Cromwell. Digby and Manuel Darquart, Jaguar, SHERELLE + Jasmine Kent-Smith, Johnno at Jockey Slut/Disco Pogo and over in Ibiza, Maya Claughton and Taryn Ross, Mark and Sarah Broadbent and Leah (Boo) Timmins and Andy Livesey.

There are way too many musicians and producers to mention but I'm going to give a very special request to Paul 'Special Request' Woolford, Armand Van Helden, James Zabiela, Sasha and John Digweed, Pete and Carolina Tong, Annie Mac, Marco 'Tensnake' Niemerski, Daft Punk, Basement Jaxx, Tom and Ed Chemical and all the original Heavenly crew, the corner toilet in The Social, everyone at The End on West Central Street especially Layo and Zoe Paskin and Matthew Bushwacka, Harry Romero + Jessica Romero + fam, Shawnee Taylor and everyone from Hackensack Plank Road, Danny Tenaglia, Sven Väth, Maurizio Schmidt, Carl and Hagi Craig, Kölsch + Julia, Ida Engberg + fam, Zoe Coe, Deep Dish, Carl Cox, Danny Howard, Sarah Story, Gilles Peterson and all at Worldwide FM, Louie and Anane Vega, Seth Troxler and Damian Lazarus, Daft Punk, Pedro Winter and Cassius (R.I.P. Philippe Zdar), Caroline Prothero and David Guetta, Jason and Emma Ellis + Elemie, Paul Weller for being a gent and to Martin L. Gore and Dave Gahan for powering my creativity via DM since '101' in 1989. R.I.P. Andrew 'Fletch' Fletcher.

To Nick Stevenson and Jerry Perkins for their unwavering support and for guiding the sleek digital and print ship into the distance.

Last but not least: thank you to The KLF for providing the perfect entry point to teenage me and for thirty years of failing safe, to Mr Andrew Weatherall who stopped me taking an early career as a data analyst.

PRE-ORDER THANKS

Thomas Baker, Jon Bills, Ian Bogg, Mark Brown, Rowena Brown, John Burgess, Naomi Cambridge, Andy Crysell, Craig Czyz, Russell Davis, Marc Dean, Michael Dingle, Sia Elenaki, Ariel Sol Faure, Lewis Fromberg, Emma Guirao, Deniz Gulyuz, Rob Hives, Christian Homan, Shona Hughes, Charlotte Jones, Si Kemp, Doug Kerr, Jasmin Khan, Johann C Kirsch, Una Kupla, Quentin Lepoutre, Alicia Lübeck, Max Lutoslawski, Jessica Mandy, Lara Marshall, Martin McNeill, Elli Michail, Colin Moore, Stevie Moore, Alice Morris, Dean Muhsin, Stuart Parkins, Benjamin Potts, Caroline Prothero, Maarten Puddy, Jack Ramage, Yvette Redmond, Dean Richmond, Edward Ryan, Philip Sagar, Wesley Saunders, Eilidh Smith, Serena Sharp, Roshan Singh, Savanna Souter, Scott Steinhardt, Shelby Stingley, John Storer, Indy Vidyalankara, Rebecca Walters, Nicola Woods

ALSO ON VELOCITY PRESS

THE SECRET DJ PRESENTS: TALES FROM THE BOOTH

The Secret DJ's first two books lifted the lid on what really happens behind the decks in the sometimes hilarious, sometimes harrowing world of the superstar DJ. Now they've reached out to dozens of DJs from around the world - and from every scene and genre – for their own true stories of the DJ life. Tales From the Booth raises the BPM, rounding up an all-star cast of Secret DJs to tell their anonymous stories of what it's really like to rock dancefloors for a living. From strange encounters on tour to side-splitting debauchery and afterparty excess to the seamy and even dangerous side of the industry, this is your access-all-areas backstage pass. You'll never look at a DJ quite the same again.

THE LABEL MACHINE
NICK SADLER

So, you want to start a record label? The Label Machine is the ultimate guide to starting, running and growing your independent record label. You will learn all about the music industry business and how to navigate the tricky dos and don'ts. You will finally understand and take control of your music copyright and get to grips with the legalities involved. You will build your label effortlessly, learning how to professionally market your music and artists – allowing you to reach thousands of fans.

TRIP CITY
TREVOR MILLER

In the summer of 1989, when *Trip City* was first released with a soundtrack by A Guy Called Gerald, there had been no other British novel like it. This was the down and dirty side of London nightclubs, dance music and the kind of hallucinogenic drug sub-culture that hadn't really been explored since Tom Wolfe's The Electric Kool-Aid Acid Test. Maybe this is why Trip City is still known as "the acid house novel" and an underground literary landmark.

But for 2021, *Trip City* is back in this all-new incendiary incarnation – including a new introduction by author Trevor Miller, a foreword by Carl Loben (*DJ Magazine* editor) and a vinyl reissue of the A Guy Called Gerald soundtrack.

LONG RELATIONSHIPS: MY INCREDIBLE JOURNEY FROM UNKNOWN DJ TO SMALL-TIME DJ
HAROLD HEATH

Written by former DJ/producer Harold Heath, Long Relationships is a biographical account of a DJ career defined by a deep love of music and a shallow amount of success. From the days of vinyl, when DJs were often also glass-collectors, to the era of megastar stadium EDM, it's a journey of 30 odd years on a low-level, economy-class rollercoaster through the ups and downs of an ever-changing music industry.

FLYER & COVER ART
JUNIOR TOMLIN

Showcasing the mastermind behind some of the most iconic rave flyers and record covers of the late eighties and early nineties, *Flyer & Cover Art* is a comprehensive insight into Junior Tomlin's incredible back catalogue.

30 years since he designed his first flyer this book documents his work across 160 pages, with commentary and draft sketches provided by Junior himself. The book is 25cm square, printed on premium 130gsm full colour paper. It is the first time his work has been documented and presented in such a comprehensive, cohesive fashion.

BEDROOM BEATS & B-SIDES: INSTRUMENTAL HIP HOP & ELECTRONIC MUSIC AT THE TURN OF THE CENTURY
LAURENT FINTONI

Bedroom Beats & B-sides is the first comprehensive history of the instrumental hip-hop and electronic scenes and a truly global look at a thirty-year period of modern music culture based on a decade of research and travel across Europe, North America, and Japan.

Combining social, cultural, and musical history with extensive research and over 100 interviews, the book tells the B-side stories of hip-hop and electronic music from the 1990s to the 2010s and explores the evolution of modern beat culture from local scenes to a global community via the diverse groups of fringe idealists who made it happen and the external forces that shaped their efforts.